IN
SEARCH
OF
THURSDAY

DIARY OF AN UNDERGRADUATE AT
THE UNIVERSITY OF VENTURE CAPITAL

PAUL TRAYNOR

First published by Talksense Books 2020

© Talksense Partners LLP
www.talksensebooks.co.uk
paul@talksensepartners.co.uk

Paperback   ISBN 978-1-8381077-0-3
eBook   ISBN 978-1-8381077-1-0

A catalogue record of this book is available from the British Library

Design by Vanessa Mendozzi

CONTENTS

FOREWORD

'What you see over there aren't giants, but windmills, and
what seems to be arms are just their sails, that go around
in the wind and turn the millstone.'
'Obviously,' replied Don Quixote, 'you don't know much
about adventures.'

Miguel de Cervantes, Don Quixote

Accidentally, my first private equity investment went to fund
a Hindu wedding. Unsurprisingly, it was a wonderful wedding
but an investment catastrophe, the first of many mishaps and
misjudgements that laid the foundation for a career in venture
capital and private equity which, given the inauspicious start, proved
surprisingly lengthy. But then, as we like to say in the venture capital
community, one's lemons ripen before one's plums.

At the age of twenty-five I decided to become a venture
capitalist. As decisions go, it has to rank as pretty heroic: I had
no background in or appetite for business or finance, I was rotten
at maths and I had no idea what venture capital was. I blame
my sister. It was she who was working at a private equity firm
and who enticed me away from a very boring administrative
job – into which I had lazily fallen post-university – with the
words: 'You put money into these little companies. They go

wrong and you have to rescue them. It's all terribly exciting.' It's still just about the best description of investing in small businesses I have ever heard.

So I joined 3i, which was an investment company known affectionately as the University of Venture Capital because it trained several generations of investment executives to become venture capital and private equity investors. This was 1985, and Silicon Valley or Wall Street would have been nice. Instead I was sent to Birmingham. I was given a car and a telephone and told to go and find some companies to invest in. They also gave me a pile of money, which I promptly lost. They didn't seem to mind, though, and gave me some more. I promptly lost that too.

For all the respectable language of high finance, putting money into companies is essentially just gambling. You find a race, assess the physique of the runner and the form of the rider, take a view of the odds, then place your bet and hold your breath while the race is run. Compared to playing the stock market, though, venture capital and private equity are *extreme* forms of gambling; in venture capital you place your bets on horses and riders with little or no form, whereas in private equity you dose up the poor animal with the monetary equivalent of cocaine (in the form of debt) in order to hype its performance. Investing is therefore, in theory at least, about learning to pick winners and shorten the odds. Those investors whose bets consistently pay out are deemed to be talented and possess superior 'commercial judgement', while those who lose money are quietly demoted and put in charge of mucking out the stables. Most of us, of course, win some and lose some and then skilfully find a way to recast the data to make ourselves appear more talented than we are. For example, if we happen to notice that we lost money on every day of the week except Thursday, we re-designate ourselves as Thursday-only investors and go again until such time as a more persuasive statistical anomaly presents itself.

This book is the story of my quest for my own personal Thursday. You're invited to join the adventure as I learn how finding an investment opportunity can be harder than flagging down a taxi at 2 a.m. on New Year's Eve, how disagreeably unscientific the process of arriving at an investment decision really is and that the best way to win deals is to do exactly the opposite of what they teach you at business school. You'll experience what it's like to gamble on the fickle fortunes of companies: the exhilaration of a big win, the terror of watching the race from behind semi-closed fingers, the despair when your horse falls at the first hurdle and the horror when the jockey decides to pocket your stake money and use it to pay for his eldest son's wedding instead. You'll meet the people too – entrepreneurs, owner-managers, management teams and the investors who move amongst them – but don't particularly expect to be awed and admiring. More often, you'll laugh, fume and occasionally hold your head in your hands in despair and disbelief.

I had to take a very circuitous route via that Hindu wedding, some very questionable investments in small enterprises and a close shave with losing £80m as a result of appalling spreadsheet skills, but my Thursday did eventually arrive in the form of the Management Buyout and, in that, my story is far from unique. Indeed, the success and prominence of the private equity industry today is almost entirely down to my generation of venture capitalists realising that management buyouts were an extraordinarily profitable bet compared with other forms of investing and piling in with increasingly huge wagers. The game therefore became not so much about picking the winners as simply finding a way to get a bet on an MBO race when so many punters were competing for a finite number of opportunities and driving the odds up to eye-watering levels. It was a game I learned to play well.

Before we start, though, I had better just explain some of the terms used in the book.

Firstly, you may already be feeling somewhat confused as to whether I'm talking about private equity or venture capital, things that are today seen as fundamentally different professions. My problem is that this distinction didn't exist in 1985. In fact the term 'private equity' wasn't an expression I even heard before the mid-1990s. Up to that point we called ourselves 'venture capitalists', although what we did was about as far away as it's possible to get from the hi-tech, chino-clad, PowerPoint-saturated, Silicon Valley image that phrase conjures up today. But we commandeered the term anyway because it felt awfully sexy. A 3i investment executive back in 1985 was a generalist, expected to be just as capable of doing a technology start-up as a growth capital investment, a management buyout or even a straight commercial mortgage. There was even a period where we were expected to sell hire purchase loans! No modern investor would dream of tackling such diversity – that would be like being asked to play football for Barcelona in the morning, rugby union for the Harlequins at lunchtime and county cricket for Kent in the afternoon before rounding the day off with a singles match at Wimbledon. This gave me something of a headscratcher when it came to the subtitle of this book. 3i was colloquially known as the 'University of Venture Capital' but most 3i 'graduates' ended up in private equity rather than venture capital so there would have been a strong case for morphing it into the 'University of Private Equity'. I suppose I could have gone for technical accuracy with the 'University of Unquoted Investment' but that's about as poetic as an investment prospectus. In the end I just stuck with 'venture capital'. More practically, in the pages that follow I've used both terms, selecting whichever one seems most appropriate in that particular context and whichever more closely reflects the practice of the time. It's all terribly confusing, I know, but you're smart people and you'll soon work it out.

A further alert regarding terminology: as you start turning the pages that follow, you will very quickly come across the strange and frequent use of the word 'controller'. This was the job title 3i gave to those of us whose role it was to find deals and manage investments. It was a thoroughly odd thing to call us, evocative of the fat top-hatted manager from Thomas the Tank Engine, slightly sinister and yet comic at the same time, and we complained about it constantly. However, the title stuck until sometime around the millennium when 3i completely reinvented itself as a conventional (and rather boring) mid-market private equity firm and distributed much more orthodox job titles amongst its investment staff, like investment executive or analyst. Ironically enough, the title of controller has now become a badge of nostalgia for those 3i alumni who so resented it back then, and I therefore persist with using it in this book. As for those of us who bore the title, it will feel strange at first but you'll soon get used to it.

Regretfully, I did not keep a diary during my time at 3i, nor did I have the foresight to retain an archive of documents. Accordingly I have had to rely heavily on memory – that faulty, mischievous and distrustful character – in reconstructing the events, deals and anecdotes related in this memoir. In a custom that would now be regarded as quaint and horrendously unproductive, we were expected to make file notes of every meeting we attended in the form of memoranda. So, throughout the book, I have used the device of the 3i Memorandum to provide some commercial detail on the investments we looked at. The 'memoranda' in this book are not real ones, however, but have all been reconstructed from memory, relying on imagination or invention to fill in the plentiful factual gaps. It is interesting how, even thirty years later, the style and clichés of the old 3i Memorandum flow as easily as if I were still producing four or five of them a day.

The 3i controller community in those days was a close, if competitive, one and most of us knew each other to some extent. Like most communities, it had its heroes and its villains, its characters and its figures of ridicule, a selection of whom appear in this book. The nature of storytelling does rather attract the narrator towards the mavericks, the rogues and the ridiculous, but it is not my intention to embarrass anyone, although I was sorely tempted to declare that anybody with a current personal net worth over £5m is fair game. I have nonetheless disguised most of the 3i characters by changing their names or substituting nicknames. For most readers this will make no difference, and for 3i alumni or those who knew 3i intimately at that time … well, you can have fun working out who is who and who is you!

So, if that has whetted your appetite, get ready to turn the page back to 1985. Margaret Thatcher is in Downing Street and Ronald Reagan in the White House. The Iron Curtain is still draped across the centre of Europe and the bricks of the Berlin wall are not yet collectable souvenirs. Even though the Communist Party of the Soviet Union has just elected Mikhail Gorbachev to be General Secretary, nobody seriously expects the cold war to end anytime soon. The Iran–Iraq War is in full swing, as is the battle for supremacy between VHS and Betamax, and – for reasons as obscure then as they are today – the French secret service sinks the Rainbow Warrior. In Britain, the first mobile phone goes on sale but only works in London, there are race riots in Brixton and the FTSE 100 stands at 1,413. Nobody has a laptop or computer screen on their desk, apart from secretaries (these days called 'personal assistants') who have exclusive access to the clunky stand-alone desktop computers known simply as 'word processors'.

Looking back at 3i through the prism of thirty-five years, there was so much to admire, plenty to astonish and a considerable amount of which to disapprove.

Boy, though, was it fun!

PROLOGUE

'It has been represented to us that great difficulty is experienced by the smaller and medium sized business in raising the capital which they may from time to time require even when the security offered is perfectly sound.'

The Report of the Committee on Finance and Industry, June 1931

Clarence Charles Hatry was, I think it's perfectly fair to say, something of a rogue.

The son of an East End silk merchant, Hatry was born in 1888 and was therefore of military age in 1914 at the start of the First World War. However, excused from military service due to a limp, the only killing Clarence was personally to be engaged in over the subsequent four years was the one he made selling personal possessions insurance to junior British officers heading off to the battlefields of northern France. Since so few of them made it back to claim for the loss of their personal effects, the ratio of premiums to claims turned out very much in Clarence's favour. After the war, Hatry went on to become something of a celebrity entrepreneur, if a rather hopeless one. By 1924 he had bankrupted no fewer than four companies, including a bank, although he nevertheless managed to emerge from each catastrophe with his personal wealth handsomely augmented. But it was his final and grandest scheme that would have consequences that reverberated around the world, the echoes of which can still be heard today.

Over the summer of 1929, Hatry cooked up a grand plan to buy up the UK and US steel industries. Despite his appalling track record, thousands of private investors flocked to invest their life savings in his company. Negotiations were begun to raise the debt required, but the banks were sceptical; the final straw came when an alert bank clerk caught Hatry forging documents and pledging the same shares as security twice over. Hatry was summoned, with his three fellow directors, to the office of the Director of Public Prosecutions of the day, the resplendently named Sir Archibald Henry Bodkin, and asked to explain himself.

Even then, Hatry couldn't resist offering a trade. He would admit to fraud and forgery, he proposed, but only on the condition that Bodkin agreed to delay the actual arrest until after lunch. Against a personal pledge from Hatry that he wouldn't abscond, Bodkin consented, allowing Hatry and his three fellow fraudsters to repair to the nearby Charing Cross Hotel where they dined extravagantly and toasted their last hours of freedom with champagne. A couple of hours later, a brace of police officers duly arrived from Scotland Yard to arrest them and transport them to jail. Rumour has it that the police sergeant who made the arrest slyly offered to allow the fraudsters to slip onto the boat train for Calais in exchange for a £20 note, but Hatry, who considered himself a man of his word, politely declined and insisted on being arrested.

This was 20th September 1929. As news of Hatry's arrest

spread, the Stock Exchange suspended trading in the shares of his company and thousands of small investors flocked to the company's offices in a futile hope that their investments could be saved. Given the trans-Atlantic nature of Hatry's grand scheme, a large number of US investors had also piled into the stock, so the contagion quickly spread to the New York Stock Exchange. Wall Street collapsed a month later, taking the US economy and that of much of the rest of the world down with it. The Great Depression that followed devastated America and Europe. In the UK alone, world trade fell by half, the output of heavy industry by a third and by 1932 there were 3.5 million unemployed.

Many factors contributed to the Wall Street Crash of 1929 and the ensuing Great Depression but the Hatry Crisis was the trigger that put them all into play. It shattered the faith investors had put in the share markets and set off the downward spiral whereby they were forced to liquidate holdings in order to pay off loans taken out to buy the shares in the first place. The presentation of that forged share certificate to Lloyds Bank was to the financial markets what the bullet of a Serbian assassin had been to the unstable system of national alliances fifteen years earlier. Hatry was the flap of the butterfly wing that led ultimately to the tornado.

It also led, fifty-seven years later, to me walking into the offices of 3i Birmingham to begin my training as a venture capitalist.

As Hatry was being transported to the Old Bailey to face trial for fraud and forgery, a very different character was in a taxi heading towards 10 Downing Street. Hugh Pattinson Macmillan was a prominent Scottish lawyer, the son of a Church of Scotland minister and a graduate in philosophy. Britain's first ever Labour government had been elected in May 1929, without even a parliamentary majority, and was clueless as to what to do in the face of economic catastrophe. So they did what all governments do and appointed a panel of experts to produce a report on it. When Ramsay MacDonald invited Macmillan to chair the inquiry, the latter protested that he knew absolutely nothing about finance or economics. 'That, my dear chap,' explained the Prime Minister drily, 'is exactly why we've chosen you.'

Throughout 1930 and the first half of 1931, a procession of famous economists trooped into austere rooms in Whitehall and presented their views. None of them agreed with each other and when the report finally appeared in June 1931, Macmillan felt honour-bound to give all the conflicting views a mention, which made the report somewhat lengthy, to say the least. When the mammoth document was finally published, it commanded the headlines for a while but was soon overtaken in the public eye by the final collapse of the Labour government and the formation of a National Government, still under MacDonald. Everybody decided that, for the time being, they had all had enough of experts and the Macmillan report was quickly forgotten.

Twelve years later, in July 1943, as the Battle of the Atlantic was reaching its climax and vast tank armies churned up blood and dust on the Russian steppes, it was unsurprising that little media attention was being paid to the formation of a committee in Whitehall tasked with thinking about post-war economic reconstruction. Above all, politicians wanted to avoid a repeat of the catastrophic recession that followed the Great War as munitions and armament industries contracted and millions of conscripted men were dumped back on the labour market. The health of the small business sector was recognised as an important component in the economic equation. Somebody on the committee remembered an obscure paragraph of just thirty-eight words that had appeared in the *Report of the Committee on Finance and Industry 1931* about the difficulties encountered by small and medium enterprises in raising long-term capital and the vague, throwaway suggestion that it might be a good idea to set up a specialist organisation devoted to plugging 'the Macmillan gap'. Like a lost mountain spring suddenly surging back to life, the idea was picked up and a proposal to create an Industrial and Commercial Finance Corporation was tabled and adopted. Its mandate would be to provide long-term capital to small and medium-sized businesses in the form of loans from £5,000 to £200,000.

ICFC, though, proved to be a bastard child. In the dark labyrinths of government, nobody quite succeeded in aborting the foetus, but nobody wanted to parent it either. The Treasury had an ideological preference for the new corporation to operate in the private sector and a less ideological preference that it not be funded with taxpayers' money. The Bank of England, expecting the project to be a commercial basket case, wanted to keep it under close supervision but wasn't prepared to fund it or run it, suggesting instead the idea of a consortium of the main UK clearing banks. The banks were appalled. They, too, thought it a commercially preposterous notion; SME's couldn't be trusted[1] with cheap money and long-term loans. It also represented a competitive threat. Why would a small business owner continue to borrow from a respectable bank when they could get a loan on more attractive terms from some upstart, politically-inspired alternative?

---

1 Small & Medium Enterprises.

However the government got its way, strong-armed the banks into providing the initial capital, gave the Bank of England a shareholding to encourage it to mediate the inevitable squabbles, and ICFC came into being. That was just the start of hostilities, though; the banks refused to offer operational support, flooded the new venture with hopeless cases passed on from local branches and tried to strangle it by supplying capital at exorbitant rates.

ICFC – cheeky, mischievous, self-reliant and innovative – refused to go under and developed an independent line of financing. To the horror of the banks, the ridiculous new venture flourished and expanded, even opening up a network of regional offices, which only served to reinforce the banks' conviction that they had been forced to spawn and subsidise a competitor – one who refused to play by the rules of the game.

I became a trainee investment controller at 3i (ICFC had changed its name to 3i a couple of years earlier) in the autumn of 1985. In that year the company made a profit of £47m and had 2,400 companies on its books, in which it had invested a cumulative total of £656m. That year alone it made 914 investments amounting to £318m. Today, 3i makes profits of £1.4bn and is listed on the London Stock Exchange with a market value of £10bn. It has been responsible for training thousands of venture capitalists and private equity investors, many of whom have gone on to create other venture capital and private equity funds across the globe. In other words, that lost mountain spring eventually grew into a truly mighty river.

Does the credit go to Hugh Pattinson Macmillan? That is the usual assertion, but it's a generous claim. Macmillan was a worthy and well-intentioned soul but those casual thirty-eight words identifying the 'Macmillan gap' only took on significance long after his report was shelved and forgotten. There is no evidence whatsoever that he, or any of the experts whose views were extensively recited in his report, ever seriously or genuinely advocated for the creation of an SME investment institution.

I very much prefer to give the credit to Clarence Charles Hatry. Without the Hatry Crisis, there may have been no Wall Street Crash, no Great Depression, no Macmillan Report, no ICFC and no career for me as a venture capitalist.

Besides, I have a soft spot for rogues, especially hopeless ones. And I have a feeling that Clarence Charles would have made an excellent 3i investment controller.

1

JOINING UP

'What day is it?' asked Pooh.
'It's today,' squeaked Piglet.
'My favourite day,' said Pooh.

A. A. Milne

July 1985
INTERVIEW DAY: 3i HEAD OFFICE, LONDON
Fortunately, nobody thinks to ask me anything difficult. Like business stuff. Or maths.

My first interview is with a tall, willowy patrician gentleman who introduces himself as a Regional Director. I have no idea what a Regional Director is but it sounds eminent and he looks old enough to be important. He uses the interview to enquire politely and extensively about strategies for getting into Oxford University. It transpires that his nephew is thinking about applying.

The second interview is with someone called Doctor Cross who is charmingly pocket-sized and, despite his name, relentlessly cheerful. He has a plaque on his door that says *Director of European Operations* so I guess he is more eminent than the last guy, who was plaqueless.

Doctor Cross notices on my CV that I hold a private pilot's licence and the reason he particularly mentions this is because he holds one too. We spend a very pleasant half hour discussing the relative flight characteristics of the Cessna 152 versus the Piper Tomahawk.

My third interview is with an intense lady who is head of Personnel Department and who quizzes me deeply and mysteriously about my relationship with my mother. Obviously I lie.

My fourth and final interview is on a different floor and is conducted by a fresh-faced, ramrod-tall Local Director who bristles with energy and is clean cut enough to have stepped out of a Mormon poster. He asks me lots of really good questions, like: 'What, in your opinion, are the three most important things to look for in a management buyout?' Which, happily for me, he then proceeds to answer himself. At the end he pumps my hand and tells me how well I've done. After escorting me to the lift, he winks as the doors close. Ugh.

By lunchtime I am out on Waterloo Road and heading back to Pall Mall where I am a very bored graduate trainee at British Aerospace. It's a meaningless and badly paid role where everybody else is over fifty and addresses each other by their surname.

Two weeks later, an offer letter from 3i drops through the letterbox. I admit I'm slightly surprised, as the interview process was so haphazard. I am excited, though. There's no question of me not accepting the offer. I'm going to be a venture capitalist. Even in those pre-Silicon Valley days, this has a certain ring about it.

It only remains for me to tell my boss at British Aerospace that I'm resigning in order to join 3i. I watch him rummage his mental database for '3i'. Suddenly he gets a hit and his eyes narrow. 'Oh! Didn't they use to be called ICFC?'

I confirm that they did.

His face screws up in disgust, as though a donkey just shat on his monogrammed British Aerospace carpet.

'But they're bloody criminals!'

That rattles me a bit. It's too late now, though. I've already accepted the offer.

Early September 1985
BIRMINGHAM

3i operates out of a network of some twenty regional offices spread across the UK. For some reason my name comes out of the hat for the Birmingham office and a date is arranged for me to travel and meet the Local Director, to whom I shall refer in this book by the nickname of Cicero.

I've never been to Birmingham before and am a bit apprehensive as it doesn't have the most positive brand as a city. I take the train up from London and I'm not exactly inspired when the seductive, cream-tea-and-scone Englishness of the Warwickshire countryside slides behind and is replaced with a haphazard littering of dilapidated factories and unkempt industrial yards. Then, as the city centre comes into view, the train lurches and dives into darkness, groaning, spitting and bellyaching. There's a hissing of brakes and the platforms of New Street Station heave to alongside, fluorescently illuminated. Rising on elevators through the concrete guts of the station complex, we spew out through the ticket barriers – a flood surge of humanity dotted with briefcases, backpacks and suitcases on wheels – into the neon light of the Bull Ring shopping centre, all discount shoe shops and aluminium shutters. There's a stink of yesterday's spices and shopper sweat.

The office is a few minutes' walk away from New Street Station in Colmore Row, which has an almost genteel air about it. 112 is an elegant Georgian townhouse squared up, like a suspect in a police identity parade, between the Bank of Scotland and the Halifax. The panelled door is wedged open and I can see there's a small porch with a glass door to the right, which leads through to a brightly lit reception. I pause for a moment or two, my heart thumping, only partly because of climbing Bennetts Hill. I step inside and push open the inner door.

Cicero is smooth as olive oil.

I'm twenty-five and spend a fair amount of our discussion trying to work out how old he is. He has a sort of neat Scandinavian look, fair skin and blue eyes, which makes him look not much older than I do. On the other hand, there's an air of authority about him that suggests he's much older. In any case, he's head of the biggest 3i office outside London, which makes him a serious player, so he can't be *that* young. He's impeccably groomed, his pinstripe suit so well-tailored that the stripes appear to flow vertically down his frame. His sentences are just as immaculately groomed as his appearance and he has this absorbing way of managing a conversation with his hands, like he's conducting a symphony orchestra in a slow waltz. It's hard to imagine him in a state of excitement, stress or anything really. He's very controlled.

I'm in his spacious office on the second floor of 112 Colmore

Row. Through a huge glass partition, we can see his personal secretary perched at her desk right outside like an alert watchdog. There's a big desk in one corner of his office but we're sitting on an L-shaped sofa positioned along the glass partition. I'm on the shorter part of the L and there's a low coffee table between us. Feeling slightly uncomfortable, I cross one leg over the other only to remember that I haven't polished my shoes in weeks. Not only is the particular shoe – now right in Cicero's eyeline – badly scuffed, but the sole has started to separate from the upper and is hanging loose like a dog's tongue. I catch him looking at it and see a tiny shard of disgust flare in his eyes, like a match being struck, before it's snuffed out. I move the offending shoe slowly from his line of sight, trying not to make it too obvious. I can see that Cicero's shoes are shinier than a Household Cavalryman's boot.

He tells me a little about how the office is organised and says he's arranged for me to meet some of the team. He's aware that I've been offered the option of a place in City Office and asks whether I have any thoughts on that. I don't really, but that seems a bit vacuous so I make something up about aspiring to work away from London and with real companies. I cringe even as it comes out of my mouth, but he doesn't embarrass me about it. He obviously intuits that I don't really know the difference between the options being offered to me because he goes on to explain that City Office is a specialist team focusing on larger and unusual transactions, often involving quoted companies and City merchant banks. Therefore the work would be very different to that in a regional office like Birmingham, where I would be working closely with small businesses. He's kind enough to precede this explanation with the preface 'As you know…', even though it's perfectly obvious that I don't. He stresses that, as long as I pick things up as quickly as he'd expect me to, I'd be working independently much earlier than at City Office and leading my own deals. He's talking to me like I'm a valued colleague rather than a prospective junior employee and I realise he's gently nudging me in exactly the direction he wants me to go, like an experienced sheepdog with an unsteady newborn lamb, but it's so skilfully done that I'm both impressed and flattered.

He wants to know if I have any questions, or would now be a good time to introduce me to some members of the team? I agree that it would. 'Good,' he says, and does this resolving gesture with his hands like he's squashing a large pillow into a small cardboard box. Despite his studied charm and diplomacy, there's something quite wolfish about Cicero.

Scotsmen are supposed to be big and bluff and that's a pretty good description of Callum, who has sandy hair and a trim moustache. Cicero effects the introductions and leaves us to talk. Callum is the current trainee controller and has been briefed to expect me. We're in a small open-plan office on the first floor, which is where the New Business Team sits. There are five desks but all the other occupants are out at meetings. Nevertheless, the place looks very much lived in, with files and papers cascading untidily over all the desks and even down onto the floors. Along the entire length of one wall there's a row of tall filing cabinets, shoulder to shoulder like guardsmen on parade, the doors of which are open to expose hundreds of green-jacketed files and buff folders suspended on racks.

Callum shows me what he's working on and explains that it's a 'Submission', which is a new and curious word to me with unfortunate undertones of deviant sexual practices occurring in discretely modified garages in the suburbs. It's a typed template on which he's handwriting amendments. I realise that a Submission is an investment paper – a request for approval for an investment. He flicks through the pages and I note with interest the content and layout: the summary of basic information about the business; the purpose of the investment; the pages of prose grouped under various headings such as Nature of Business, Management, and Trading Information, along with the financial data at the end; a profit and loss account; a balance sheet and a cashflow. With relief I realise that it looks really quite obvious and doable.

I like Callum. He's sound and down to earth and there's not a trace of arrogance about him. He gives me a brief rundown on life as a controller in 3i Birmingham and fills me in on the rest of the team. In addition to the New Business Team, there's a Portfolio Team living on the third floor and some 'girls', by which he means secretaries, who work in separate rooms at the front of the building. Cicero occupies a spacious office all to himself on the second floor. There's another 'Local Director', Clump, who reports to Cicero but manages the New Business Team and who sits in the front office on the first floor. Something makes me think Callum doesn't think too highly of Clump, but he doesn't say anything specific.

We chat for a few minutes and then he says he expects to be finished with his Submission in an hour or so. He's already arranged for himself and some other members of the team to take me to the pub. Sounds good to me.

It's nearly three o'clock and four pints later before I'm on the train back to London, feeling more than a little woozy. Callum had taken me to the Shakespeare's Arms, a grubby pub under the ramp from New Street Station along which I'd descended just a couple of hours before and where we were joined by a steady stream of other controllers, plus some of the 'girls'. I should have been full of questions about the job but to be honest I was struggling to think of any so I just relaxed into the banter and the chat. Everyone seemed very grounded and easy going, and seemed to enjoy poking absurdities at each other and at the favoured object of their wit and cynicism: 3i management.

As I drift off into an inebriated snooze, I can't help thinking that this all feels really, really great. There's no question of wanting to join City Office. It's Birmingham for me.

October 1985

My new employment contract starts on 1st October but, since I have no accountancy training, I have to spend the first three weeks doing an accounting course at some featureless accounting college in Kensington. It's painfully dull but at least I get to stay in a proper hotel just off Hyde Park.

I'm still not far enough out of being a student that I don't get a thrill at being put up in a smart hotel. There's a minibar, although the prices are so exorbitant I daren't actually consume anything from it, an executive desk with leather chair and soft porn films available for rent on the hotel film channel – although I'm far too fearful of *The Adventures of Misty Beethoven* or *Lezzes in Latex* appearing on the invoice to risk watching any. There's also a prostitute stationed permanently near the lifts, although the individual girl changes according to some kind of rota. Needless to say, I live in terror of being accosted whilst at the same time thinking that the least they could do is *ask*. Don't they know I'm a *venture capitalist*? That has to be worth a proposition, surely. Which naturally I would shrug off with grace and indifference, because being solicited by escorts is the sort of thing that happens to us venture capitalists all the time. Anyway, we're not exactly talking about sophisticated courtesans here. One lady in particular is intimidatingly vast, while nevertheless strapped into the clingiest and skimpiest of orange leather miniskirts. I would have thought a venture capitalist would be a prize catch for these girls but, to be fair, there's no way for them to know, really. In another ten years I will be stepping out of the lift, ostentatiously concluding some massive deal over the phone, but mobiles haven't been invented yet. So, for the time being, I have to make do with strutting out of the lift in an unambiguously venture-capitalist sort of way.

They still don't pay me any attention. Probably for the best, though, eh?

> Question 10: 'Calculate the net profit, net of a 10% bonus for the manager, after taking account of such bonus.'

We're being tested on what we're supposed to have learned so far, but this is doing my head in. Is that the same as 90% of the net profit? It feels like a trick question, but maybe it's not, and I'm glad they didn't throw little tests like this at me during the interview. Fortunately, I'm sitting next to an investment banker who has a degree in Maths and is trading answers in exchange for pints in the pub later.

The next day I get a violent stomach disorder and can't leave the hotel room. I call in sick and 3i send a private doctor to the hotel. I'm not sure whether this is because they are committed to outstanding care for their employees or because they suspect

I am shirking. Probably the latter. The doctor takes a sample and calls me the next day to say I picked up a nasty bug during my recent white-water rafting trip to Nepal. He's arranged for the antibiotic equivalent of a ten-kiloton nuclear bomb to be delivered direct to my hotel room and in the meantime I am NOT to risk passing on the infection to anybody else.

I'm stuck in the hotel room for ten days watching *The Italian Job* and *Oliver!* on a constant loop as, other than *Misty Beethoven* and *Lezzes in Latex*, they are the only two films available on the hotel film channel. Soon the dialogue merges into my stream of consciousness and I find catchphrases from the films randomly popping up in my head.

You were only supposed to blow the bloody doors off.

I make it back to the accounting course for the last few days. We've moved on to the intricacies of accounting for sinking funds. What? What even is a sinking fund? I find myself imagining a large container filled with cash and abandoned off the coast of Ibiza, much to the horror of crowds of inebriated, cash-strapped partygoers lining the rails of passing disco cruise liners. My imagination does not quite stretch to explaining why on earth anybody should *wish* to sink a large fund of cash into the depths of the Mediterranean Sea but, if they did, I would have thought accounting for it would be fairly straightforward. I'm not entirely sure what the relevance of all this is for my future career in venture capital except that the word *sinking* hardly seems propitious.

In this life, one thing counts. In the bank, large amounts.

Seems rather appropriate.

The course finally winds up and, to my relief, there doesn't seem to be any examination to pass. I've got the basics of profit and loss accounts and balance sheets. The rest I'll pick up on the job.

There's only a weekend now between me and becoming a venture capitalist. I'm getting imposter syndrome already. A few of my future colleagues had been on the course and they all seemed scarily knowledgeable and confident. None of them are coming to Birmingham though. The next time I see them will be on one of the internal training courses.

I'm planning to drive up on Sunday afternoon, even though I could get up ultra-early on Monday and still make it to the office for a reasonable time. But I don't want to take the risk of being delayed and making a bad first impression. I want to avoid getting caught up in the late-night Sunday traffic and leave London about 3 p.m. The drive up the M1 is nevertheless pretty busy but eases when I take the branch off onto the M6.

Spaghetti Junction is a doddle compared to the ring road around Birmingham City Centre. 3i have arranged for me to stay in the Holiday Inn until I can rent somewhere; the hotel passes me high on the left, then high on the right, then high on the left again and I still can't see how to get to it. I've invested in a brand-new *A to Z* of Birmingham and keep having to pull over to consult it. What I really need is a TomTom satnav but it's at least another twenty years before they will be invented, so I have to make do and improvise. I end up driving along desolate streets surrounded by run-down buildings and rubble-strewn open spaces, with the Holiday Inn somehow always visible but persistently inaccessible. Whatever its commercial possibilities, Birmingham is not an attractive place.

Later, alone in my executive single room, I eat a salty Chinese takeaway and feel a sort of gnawing emptiness inside. I'm not

sure whether it's trepidation or excitement.
Or maybe it's just the Chinese.

2

LEARNING TO BOUNCE

3i is a company whose business is investment. We offer a distinct blend of financial and industrial skills which help develop successful businesses. We invest in companies from small start-ups through growing businesses to major national and international concerns. We have held investments in many of these companies for more than 20 years, although many float in 7.

3i Group Annual Report, March 1986

First Week
Needless to say, when in late October 1985 I walk back into the office on 112 Colmore Row to begin my training as an investment controller, the most sophisticated blender in the world would struggle to produce anything nutritious from the sparse ingredients that comprise my personal portfolio of financial and industrial skills.

I have everything to learn. But that's okay – I'm there *to* learn. And whilst I am under no illusion about my inexperience or ignorance, I have absolutely no doubt that very soon I will personally be the catalyst of success for an entire generation of rapt, admiring and deeply grateful entrepreneurs. I am twenty-five years old, an Oxford graduate, brimming with energy and possibility. The world of venture capital is waiting for me.

In particular, I'm really looking forward to finding out exactly what venture capital is.

When you start a new job, you notice lots of odd and weird things.

'Odd things' are things that seem odd to begin with but start to make sense after they've been explained to you.

Like why all the controllers are always pacing up and down the office muttering into their fists.

Like why all the internal company memos are printed off in blue, green or pink.

Like why we're called 'controllers'.

'Weird things' are things that never make sense but after a while you get so used to them you stop realising how weird they are.

Like how we call the companies we invest in 'customers'.

Like how, for a company that says its business is to invest, we seem to spend the vast majority of our time saying we don't want to. It's a bit like being a doctor and turning patients away because they are ill.

Like how everyone talks about 'deals' rather than 'investments'.

Like how we always demand to see a business plan before we meet a company but then never bother to read it until after the meeting has happened.

The phones are constantly ringing with people wanting money. For some reason we call them GEs.

I'm given a desk in the New Business office where there are

five desks and four experienced controllers, including Callum. The office is open plan specifically to enable controllers to listen in to each other's conversations, which feels odd at first. At my previous employer, this would have been called eavesdropping and been frowned upon. The idea is to encourage teamwork and to provide the junior members of staff (that's me) with an opportunity to pick things up. So my first exposure to the world of venture capital is listening to half-conversations.

What strikes me straight away is that the average telephone GE seems to have a lifespan shorter than a mayfly at the height of summer.

We say no because the amount is too small.

We say no because the company is too small while the amount of capital they want is too large.

We say no because the company won't ever be successful.

We say no because there isn't any financial information.

We say no because the caller is annoying and clearly a dickhead.

I am soon assembling an impressive list of reasons for not doing an investment.

If an entrepreneur successfully navigates this archipelago of jagged coral objections without a fatal hole being torn in the hull of his entrepreneurial project, he is invited to send in a business plan for consideration. Judging by what I witness over the first few days, it's going to be a while before I get to see one of those.

Saying no to a GE is called 'bouncing' and it's the first thing I have to learn to do.

Clump heads up the New Business Team. He's a Local Director but not a real one. Real ones, like Cicero, have a whole regional office to themselves, like Birmingham or Manchester or Edinburgh or Brighton. (Brighton? Seriously? We have an office in Brighton? Why on earth would we have an office in Brighton?). Making it to become a real Local Director is a really big thing – everybody wants to be one.

Clump is a tall, fleshy man with the pouched cheeks of a hamster; his eyes flick constantly around, like he's saying one thing but thinking another. He bustles incessantly, stirred by a restless energy, and he talks at you with the sincerity of a hotel manager greeting a new guest. He's constantly calling people through to his office to check up on the progress of this deal or that, or sweeping into the front office with a fresh business plan under his arm like a portly emperor penguin turning up at the nest with a juicy fat fish for the chicks to clamour over. Clump likes to advertise his membership of an obscure Christian sect that spurns worldly affairs. The controllers think this is funny because Clump is the dodgiest character they know.

In addition to Callum, there are four other controllers on the New Business Team: Salty, Dabble, Bunny and Windmill. Salty is cast from the same mould as Callum – friendly, helpful and always ready with a quip or a joke. Dabble is a bit older, and irritable, with a tendency to screw up his face when he's sceptical about something, which seems to be most of the time. Bunny is bespectacled, big and round, a fountain of professional positivity with a faint air of chivalry about him. Windmill is a lot older than everyone else; nobody knows for sure, but there's a rumour he's already over forty – impossibly ancient for a controller. Despite his age, he still has the look of a handsome teenager – though without the acne – with a chipmunk face and a set of perfectly even white teeth, which glint at you like a toothpaste advert when he grins.

I'm allocated to Dabble as my 'mentor', which means he's to

show me the ropes and supervise my training. Salty is perceptive enough to notice my disappointment and finds a moment to take me aside and confide, somewhat obscurely, that Dabble is an accountant. Apparently there's a clear cultural distinction down the office between accountants and graduates, like the football and rugby teams at school. The accountants are the snobby rugby players in posh cotton kit, while the graduates are the unsophisticated, unruly football players wearing nylon.

In addition to Clump and the controllers there are two secretaries. Alex is a bubbly, very attractive girl who can't be more than twenty-one, while Jo is a sharp Australian blonde in her early thirties who likes to be the subject of rumours of scandalous carnal relationships with married cricketing and footballing celebrities, although she is widely suspected of starting these rumours herself. They have Wang word processors on their desks and, since this is long before executives have email or even personal computers, they spend most of their time typing. No wonder they are permanently bored.

On the third floor – largely out of sight – are the Portfolio Team, whose prime responsibility is to look after the investments we have already made. The team there is headed up by a senior controller rather than a Local Director and it takes me no time at all to work out that, despite working two floors above us, we in the New Business Team look down on the Portfolio Team.

It seems that controllers who find and do deals are like the strikers in a football team. They create opportunities and score the goals and that's what matters. The Portfolio Team are like the defenders; they do an important job but everyone knows they *really* want to be strikers. However, we all have to pretend out loud that the two jobs are equivalent in status so as not to demotivate the Portfolio Team.

Deals are a constant topic of conversation.

Controllers are given cash out targets, which is the amount they're supposed to invest in a year. A controller is expected to do at least four deals a year and, since the average size of a typical investment is around £150,000, that means that he (or, more rarely, she) is likely to have a cash out target of at least £600,000. For the more senior guys who are expected to do bigger deals, the target might reach £1m-2m.

One thing already becoming clear is that 3i has a voracious appetite for cash out. We want to put as many deals on the books as possible and get as much cash out the door as we can. The people who win respect around here are the 'dealers', the controllers who find deals and get them done.

Before I joined, I honestly hadn't thought about it at all. Where do *deals* come from? I had done a fair bit of fantasising about shrewdly and swiftly assimilating a business proposition, the entrepreneur wilting a little under my penetrating interrogation, but the fantasy had never extended to *finding* the deals – in my imagination they were just somehow *there*.

It's therefore a bit of a shock to discover that deals don't just materialise. You have to go out and find them. And they're scarce.

I learn that all the really good deals come to us via a tiny group of very active advisers, who are either local accountants or solicitors who charge the company a fee for helping them to raise finance. These key relationships tend to be controlled by Cicero and Clump, to whom the introductions go. Cicero and Clump then allocate the business plans to the controllers, like food parcels tossed to starving refugees out of the back of an aid lorry. The best and biggest deals go to the most experienced and effective controllers. Junior controllers, and certainly trainees, don't get a look in. Why would they? If a good deal comes in you want to put your best and most experienced on it.

In a large patch like the West Midlands, there are of course hundreds, probably thousands, of accountants and solicitors, a lot of whom work in mid-sized or smaller firms. There's always a chance that one of these will come across a deal, perhaps involving a client they have on their books, so they need to be marketed to and made aware of our interest. But marketing to secondary advisers is a low-yield business: it requires a lot of time (and a lot of lunches) and is unlikely to produce an actual deal. Even if it does, the deal will probably be smaller and more difficult to do.

The next potential source of deals is GEs: people who approach us, usually in the form of a telephone call, although sometimes they send in an unsolicited business plan or, infrequently, just walk in off the street. Occasionally a good deal will come in by GE but it's like hunting for discarded jewellery in the council tip: you have to sieve through an awful lot of rubbish to find anything that gleams. Most GEs haven't a clue what we do, so we get approached by everyone for everything – from self-employed bricklayers wanting an advance for the weekend, to launderettes, hairdressers, cafés, golf courses, shops and restaurants. We also get lots of people who have just had a 'great idea for a business', usually inventors of an allegedly clever product like a new type of umbrella or a widget for storing food. Trivial Pursuit has a lot to answer for as we get people who are convinced they have designed the next great board game to sweep the dinner party world. God knows where these people get our telephone number from. Walk-in GEs are acknowledged to be the worst.

The vast majority of the calls we get, though, are from established – albeit small – businesses who have just heard of us somehow or, in many cases, have been referred to us by their bank. Most bank managers are equally clueless as to what we do, but when they turn an SME customer down for an increased overdraft or a loan, they like to be seen as helpful and point them in our direction. Very few of these companies are big enough or interesting enough for us to want to invest in them.

Last of all there's cold calling. Otherwise known as the telephone directory. We're supposed to be active and call up businesses, get through to the managing director and persuade him (or, very rarely, her) to agree to a meeting. Everyone hates cold calling and regards it as a complete waste of time, but for political purposes we are expected to pretend that it's a wholesome and essential element of a 'strategic' marketing programme. (I learn that the word *strategic* is the corporate equivalent of a vaccine – something injected into a statement to immunise it against cynicism). Recognition is supposedly given to controllers who are perceived to be active and energetic cold callers.

Marketing goes with hierarchy: the senior controllers get to market to the best advisers, the established controllers get the secondary advisers and the trainee gets the GEs and the cold calling.

I don't mind fielding telephone calls but the idea of calling complete strangers and trying to sell them things fills me with abject horror. What happened to 'helping successful businesses with a distinct blend of financial and industrial skills'? Nobody told me I was going to be a telecalls salesman.

Learning how the office works and listening in to telephone calls is all very well, but I'm keen to meet some real customers and see how a deal is done. Callum obliges by inviting me to accompany him to a meeting.

We're soon racing through the back streets of Birmingham in Callum's Mini Metro Turbo. It's a pool car because, as a trainee, he's not yet entitled to a company car and he expresses his contempt for this outrage by trying to blow up the engine, gunning it until a row of florid green lights flickers across the dashboard as the turbo allegedly engages. 'Sounds like a ball bearing in a fucking biscuit tin', he growls, his big bluff Scottish head squashed up against the roof of the tiny car so hard he has to tilt it. As we left the office he had jammed some papers into my hand that the company sent in ahead of the meeting, telling me to read them on the way. It looks like a rudimentary business plan but the way Callum is flinging the car around the roundabouts is making me feel sick so I just hold on to it with clammy hands and snatch glances when we stop at the occasional traffic light. Callum notices.

'Ach, don't worry. Haven't read it myself yet.'

'Oh! Isn't that ... well ... awkward?' I almost said 'unprofessional' but changed it at the last second.

He barks out a laugh.

We pull into an industrial estate and consult a signpost, in a state of considerable disrepair, with the names and unit numbers of the businesses located on the estate. The roads through the estate are bounded by shabby single-storey industrial units and there's a mobile café advertising hot tea and 'full English'. We locate the unit we're looking for, which looks as run-down as all the rest, and park in one of the bays outside. A Jaguar X-type, which looks reasonably new, is parked in a bay designated

Chairman and Managing Director. When we open the car doors we're assailed by the sweet smell of frying onions from the mobile café.

Glamorous this isn't. But I'm not bothered by that. This is obviously what we do and I'm buzzing with curiosity and anticipation.

The entrance has a sign that someone has printed off on plain white paper and sellotaped to the window, saying *'NO SALESMEN WILL BE SEEN WITHOUT PRIOR APPOINT-MENT'.* There's no reception, just a small, vacant room with a couple of plastic chairs and a low coffee table on which are strewn a handful of dog-eared magazines with titles like *Engineering Today,* and a telephone with a sticker that says *Dial 0 for Assistance.* Callum picks up the phone, dials, and announces our presence.

A few minutes later an inner door pushes open and the managing director greets us with handshakes. He looks a little uncomfortable in his suit. He speaks with a broad Brummie twang and suggests we 'do the tour' before going to his office for a 'chat'. The 'tour' starts in the main part of the unit where two squat CNC machines[2], each as big as Callum's Mini Metro Turbo, are competing to out-squeal and out-clatter each other. As we approach we can see they are performing some sort of cutting operation, involving a lump of metal rotating against a cutting tool. Each machine has an operator, wearing plastic goggles and a stained boiler suit, who is monitoring the machine and occasionally punching some new numbers into a plastic panel. It's actually quite hypnotic watching the lump of steel

---

2 Computer Numerically Controlled.

being carved, cut and caressed, like watching a clay pot take shape under the hands of a skilled potter. There's a smell of hot machine oil and recently worked metal. Beside each machine is a packing case into which the operator is throwing the finished product, a steel cylinder several inches long with various ridges. Our host picks one up and explains, with liberal use of hand gestures, that it's a component for a shock absorber. Hanging on the frame of the CNC machine and all over the walls and noticeboards are numerous calendars with pictures of female models posing topless. It's evidently business-critical that the workforce remain constantly up to speed as to which day of the week it is.

The tour takes us into a back office, introduced to us as the 'Accounts Department', that contains five people and an awful lot of box files. The staff all look up and acknowledge us shyly. Then we're into the MD's office. He's about to take up position behind his desk when he notices that there's only one chair between Callum and I, so he goes back out to the accounts office to fetch one.

He opens the discussion by asking if we got the papers he sent over.

'Yes, thanks,' says, Callum, 'very interesting and impressive! But why don't you just tell us about the business in your own words?'

It seems transparent to me that Callum hasn't read the documents that our host has taken the trouble to send in beforehand, but the MD doesn't seem in the least insulted and proceeds to talk at length without saying anything at all. A lot of his meandering monologue seems to be concerned with 'quality', as though quality is an actual thing in itself. His formless discourse never quite arrives, though, at a point of enlightenment as to what 'quality' is or how it applies to his business.

Callum lets this go on for what feels like an interminable time, then interrupts to drag the conversation over to the financial performance of the company. I realise that he's been profiting from the MD's loquaciousness by surreptitiously glancing at the business plan. It seems the accounts show marginal profits on sales of half a million. The MD explains that he's thinking of buying some more CNC machines in the hope of securing new work from British Leyland, but the bank's not sympathetic. At least we seem to be getting somewhere.

During the meeting, the MD's phone rings constantly and, to my astonishment, he picks up and engages in a lengthy conversation with the caller, apparently oblivious to our presence. I think it's bloody rude, but Callum doesn't make anything of it. As a result the meeting takes forever. It's like playing in a football match where the centre forward goes down injured every five minutes, obliging the rest of the team to stand around waiting for play to resume. The MD doesn't seem concerned about time, though, and I get the impression he's rather enjoying being the centre of attention and having us wait on him. Eventually Callum manages to bring the meeting to a conclusion and we leave, promising to get back to him within a few days with 'our thoughts'.

In the car on the way back Callum asks me what I think. I'm vague and non-committal because I don't know what *to* think. Is this what we do? For all I know that was either a brilliant investment opportunity or a complete waste of time. I really have no idea. I ask Callum what he thinks and he says it's a deal we probably would have done five years ago, but now … 'Ach. I just don't see where the upside is.' I don't know what *upside* means but am too embarrassed to ask so I just nod sagely like that was *exactly* what I was thinking myself. I wonder, too, in what way things were different five years ago.

Nevertheless, this is clear progress. At least I now have something to enter on the positive side of the balance sheet for what to look for in a deal. With a flourish I mentally inscribe the words 'must have upside' on my expanding template of investment criteria. It looks a bit lonely there on that side, opposite all those reasons for saying no, but I'm sure I'll be adding to it soon.

I'm deeply envious of the way Callum dismisses the deal with such devastating nonchalance: *I just don't see where the upside is.* That's so cool. I can't wait until I can do that too.

On Friday, as if as a reward for lasting a whole week, Dabble lets me handle a telephone GE. Callum and Salty are at their desks, pretending not to pay attention, but I can tell they're tuning in expecting entertainment. Dabble is listening in on the other phone.

The caller tells me he owns a very successful building supplies business in Willenhall. Business is very brisk, apparently. He goes into some detail about what his top selling products are and shares anecdotes, which seem intended to impress me with his business acumen. Politely, I wait for him to reach a conclusion – perhaps, for example, by stating the reason for his call? But the voice meanders on with no obvious destination in sight. Dabble catches my eye and makes fast little circles with his index finger, indicating that I need to move him along. I decide to run down my checklist for saying no but I have to interrupt three times before he will even give a direct answer to the basic question of how much he is looking to raise.

'Well, the bank manager says it would be good if we could reduce the overdraft a bit. Say £20,000?'

'You're looking to raise £20,000? To repay the bank overdraft?'
Gotcha. The amount is too small. He's hit the very first reef
and I hear the metaphorical sound of the hull ripping in his
entrepreneurial project and the glug-glug of seawater rushing in.

'I'm sorry but that's below our investment threshold.'

'Oh okay. So, what's your threshold?'

I see Dabble shaking his head emphatically and wagging his
finger to say 'No, don't go there.'Too late; I've already answered.

'Our minimum investment size is £50,000.'

'Alright.'

'What?'

'I said that would be alright. Probably better in fact, now I
think about it. We can pay off the entire overdraft and have a
bit left over for a rainy day.'

'No, that's not ... I mean – NO! I'm not *offering* you £50,000.
I'm just saying the amount you're looking to raise is below our
minimum investment threshold.'

'Yeah. No. I got that. So, I'll take the £50,000 then.'

'NO! Sorry, it doesn't work like that. You can't ring up and ask
for £20,000 and then a few minutes later just up it to £50,000.'

'Why not?'

Dabble is fighting to stop a snort of hilarity getting out,
which just ends up with his face contorting into a passable
imitation of someone sucking on a rancid lemon. It's good to
know someone is enjoying this.

This isn't quite what I envisaged with 'helping develop
successful businesses.' It's more like trying to stamp on a
cockroach. And about as effective. No matter how hard you
stamp, when you lift your foot the bugger is somehow still alive.

I'm being taught the first and most important lesson in
venture capital: when bouncing a GE, *never ever* give a reason

because that reason just becomes a hurdle for them to clear. And no matter how high you think you've set the hurdle, they'll just withdraw a few steps, take a deep breath, and have another run at it. If you say the amount is too small, they'll just ask for more; if you say they're not profitable enough, the accounts will come back showing more profit; if you say the market is too competitive, the next day you'll receive a suitcase of newspaper articles arguing exactly the opposite.

The problem, though, is how to say no without giving a reason. I'm a well-educated person and I've spent the last twenty years of my life learning that giving vague, unhelpful answers to specific questions gets you a fail. Now it seems the first new skill required in this venture capital business is to learn to blow smoke. This turns out to be a lot harder than it sounds. I'm stumped: complete brain freeze.

Fortunately, Dabble breaks into the conversation and bails me out. Smoothly, he thanks the gentleman for his call but, despite what I had said, there is no set minimum threshold, just a need to weigh the potential upside against the risks in each individual case. 'Taking into account the relatively small sum of money involved, and the overall competitiveness of the market, not to mention the current economic outlook … looking at it in the round, it's not a situation we would invest in.' His tone is firm but his explanation is vague and contains absolutely nothing the caller can wrestle with. So that's how you do it. The guy, perhaps also a bit discombobulated by the change of personnel mid-call, grumpily concedes and the conversation ends.

Dabble and I put our telephones back on the hook and he says, 'You did well.' But he's just being supportive because he knows that's what he's supposed to do.

'Just for your information, by the way … we never invest to

pay out the bank.'

I add that one to the list.

It's early days, I know, but we are yet to cover what happens when a GE somehow successfully navigates the infernal archipelago of reasons to say no. The danger is that I'll end up having to invent a new reason to say 'no', because I don't yet know what happens when they get a 'yes'.

I'm developing a metaphor for what we do.

Think of the traffic in a busy city. The vehicles are companies, the drivers are the managers and business owners, and there are often – but not always – passengers in the form of financiers: shareholders and bankers.

The shareholders sit in the front seat alongside the managers, while the bankers only get to sit in the back.

In every city there are thousands of journeys taking place every day, the vast majority of which you will never know about and which, as a venture capitalist, won't concern you. But there's a particular subset of journeys where the vehicle is going to be much more valuable at the end of the journey than at the beginning. Is there a way you can earn some of that value? In many cases the driver and passengers don't need your money (or blend of financial and industrial skills) to undertake the journey, so there's nothing to be done. But in *some* cases, the driver doesn't have enough cash to fund the petrol required and even a whip around amongst the passengers doesn't produce enough. As a VC, this is your opportunity. You pop up, offer to contribute to the petrol kitty and, in return, demand a share of the value of the vehicle when it's sold at the end of the journey. And, just to make sure of collecting your money, you hop in alongside the driver, from where you can freely give directions and offer your invaluable commentary on the driver's handling skills.

Of course, you have to find and identify these particular journeys first and, since they are a tiny proportion of the overall journeys being made at that point in time, that's not straightforward. Finding deals is called *marketing*. And then, when you find a journey that interests you, you have to persuade the driver to take you along rather than the horde of other venture capitalists who are surrounding him like a mob of sycophantic journalists baying around a new royal baby. Persuading a company to do the deal with you rather than someone else is called *selling*.

And believe me, as an aspiring venture capitalist, there is nothing more frustrating than watching a deal cruise past you with another venture capitalist in the passenger seat, nose pressed against the glass, grinning at you and flicking the finger.

Especially when it's somebody who works for the same company as you.

What do you think? Good metaphor? I like it so much I share it with Cicero. He says it's not a metaphor; it's an analogy.

Controllers tend not to stay around for long. They move to other offices, get promoted to become Local Directors or leave to join other venture capital funds. New firms are mushrooming up everywhere and existing ones are growing fast; they all need trained investment executives and the best place to obtain them is from the University of Venture Capital. It's like a convection system – fresh air gets sucked in at the bottom and rises to replace the hot air escaping at the top. A constant influx of new controllers is therefore needed to avoid a vacuum occurring. So 3i relies on recruiting young people with no experience and training them fast and in sufficient numbers to replace the experienced ones moving up or leaving. Some of that training can be done in the classroom but there really is no substitute for finding and negotiating a deal.

But there's a catch 22: to be given a shot at a quality deal you have to be an experienced and proven dealer. But to become an experienced and proven dealer you need to have a shot at a quality deal. Unfortunately, until you are proven, all you get to look at is crap.

Inevitably, therefore, the first deals you do are the riskiest ones and the most likely to go wrong. The nature of the investment business is that, if you're lucky, it may be quite a while before they go wrong, by which time you'll have moved onwards and upwards. Inconveniently, though, the investments that go wrong generally have a habit of going wrong quickly while those that succeed take a long time to do so. In investment terms this is called *one's lemons ripening before one's plums*. Over time it's obviously very important to build a reputation as a plum grower rather than a lemon ripener. Having said that, being good at producing plums is not the only way to achieve a reputation as a good investor. For example, since investments are constantly being redistributed around different controllers, there's a perfectly effective cuckoo strategy whereby you appropriate other people's plums, tut loudly to indicate how very lemony they are and then miraculously convert them back into juicy plums by virtue of your outstanding commercial skills. Conversely, you can also disown any lemons you may have been responsible for by asserting that they were perfectly healthy plums when you bequeathed them to the next controller.

When you observe this strategy in action, which you certainly will, it is customary to smile whimsically whilst intoning: *success has many fathers but failure is a bastard.*

It's a shame, really, that we haven't yet been approached by an entrepreneur who's discovered a way to change one sort of citrus fruit into another. It would get funded in a heartbeat.

What all this means is that 3i, which trains the whole industry, has a tacit acceptance that trainees are almost certainly going to lose money on their first few deals. This is referred to colloquially as the 'Training Budget'. Since we are the only firm training investors, and because so many people leave after only a year or two, we are effectively funding the Training Budget for the entire industry, which is very generous.

The real problem, though, is that if you spend your entire life looking at crap and crap alone, some of it actually starts to look quite good.

My first week as a venture capitalist is over and Friday afternoon finishes with drinks in Cicero's office at 4 p.m. After consuming several generous gin & tonics, a group of us detach and continue at the Old Contemptibles, which runs a Happy Hour from 5 p.m. to 7 p.m. on Friday night. You get two shots for the price of one. Given the generosity of this offer, we are prepared to overlook the mathematical oversight of a Happy Hour that carries on for two. I don't get back to the hotel until after midnight and I'm so pissed I can barely get the key in the door of my room.

3

FIRST ENCOUNTERS

'In this life one thing counts.
In the bank, large amounts.
Large amounts, they don't grow on trees.
You've got to pick a pocket or two, boys!'

Fagan, from Oliver!

Second Week

Monday mornings start promptly at 8:30 with a WIP meeting. WIP stands for 'work in progress', which means we go through a list of current and completed deals. GE's, I now learn, stands for 'general enquiries'.

Cicero chairs it and the whole team attends, except for secretaries. Clump takes up position opposite Cicero while Salty, Dabble, Callum and Bunny distribute themselves around the large boardroom table. Windmill comes in last. The Portfolio Team are also present, comprising Speedcheck (the team leader), Anne and Banter. Speedcheck seems a dry character, particularly in comparison with Clump. He has the sinewy physique of a whippet and gives off an air of being permanently pissed off about something. Anne is the only female controller and has a nobody-messes-with-me attitude. The final controller is Banter, with a shock of black wiry hair, a complexion that looks like he's been freshly drained overnight by a vampire and a cadaverous laugh. Cicero circulates a printout and we all come to order, flicking through it.

It shows a list of current deals and it's immediately obvious that this is really a sales meeting. The company's name and the amount of capital involved are listed by controller, so you are instantly confronted by a statement of who's doing the business. Callum has by far and away the most deals to his name, Salty and Bunny are some way behind, while Dabble has just a few. The Portfolio Team has some entries as well but they're marked with an 'S' for 'subsequent', which means a top-up loan to, or share subscription in, a company into which we have already invested. These are treated respectfully, but there's a definite sense that they don't carry the same weight as a new investment.

Cicero starts the meeting by pointing me out and inviting everyone to welcome me. There are a few courteous nods and half-smiles, and I feel I ought to say something self-assured and impressive until I realise that no one cares. I'm just the new trainee. Cicero announces 'New Business' and looks at Clump, who picks up the WIP sheet and starts going through the deals and asking questions, throwing his weight around a bit, cajoling the controllers to sort this out or get a move on with that. We're over halfway through our financial year for which our cash out target is £20m. We've only done £6m to date, putting us a bit behind track. On the other hand we're well ahead of the same period last year, but Clump is quick to emphasise that none of us should be satisfied with that.

Frankly, given what I was witness to in my first week, I am cheered to see that we're actually doing deals. A germ of a suspicion had been forming in my mind that there must be a hidden room somewhere in the building where the real venture capitalists work.

I can't quite work out the relationship between Cicero and Clump. Clump is exaggeratedly deferential towards Cicero in a way that drips insincerity, while Cicero treats Clump with fastidious courtesy. They don't seem like a team to me.

For internal 3i use only
3i MEMORANDUM

From: **Paul Traynor**
To: **File**
Date: **12th November 1985**
Subject: **Stirchley Automotive Components Limited**
Cc: **Callum XXXX**

CX and PT visited this company at its premises in Stirchley.

The company makes turned parts for the automotive industry, principally components for shock absorbers, using two CNC machines. The company's major customer is British Leyland (Vans Division) which accounts for two-thirds of its current sales. The remaining third of sales is distributed across a range of other customers.

The company is 100% owned by Chairman & Managing Director Thomas Parke (although half of the shares are in his wife's name). Thomas is an experienced and sensible engineer who has been running the business for over 15 years. He clearly has a good relationship with Leyland Vans but has struggled to grow the business either through additional customers or new products.

The company is only just profitable, having made a net profit of just £18k in calendar 1984 on revenues of £534k. That was a small improvement on the prior year but the accounts show no real progress for at least the last few years. The balance sheet is weak, with negligible reserves and borrowing at the last balance sheet date of c.£40k of which £30k is overdraft and £10k of outstanding hire purchase commitments on the CNC machines. The bank overdraft facility is £30k, secured principally by a floating charge over trade debtors.

The company is looking for investment of £75k-£100k for working capital and to finance the purchase of two additional CNC machines. Parke believes that, with the additional capacity, he will be able to win some profitable new business with alternative Tier 2 automotive suppliers, improving profitability and reducing the company's dependence on Leyland Vans.

While Parke seemed commercial and conservative his ability to secure profitable new business remains fundamentally unproven. The company is currently stable and profitable but, particularly in light of the excessive short-term borrowing, has to be considered especially vulnerable to a potential loss of the Leyland business or even just a general downturn in the economy.

I called Parke to inform him that, on balance, this was not one for 3i.

It's my first ever file memo and I spend hours crafting it. Every meeting has to be documented with a memo to file.

Since a team of so many controllers implies a *lot* of meetings, we generate an enormous number of memos. The standard practice is to dictate the documents into a Dictaphone, then hand the tape to the girls for typing. The Dictaphone is what the controllers are always muttering into. Each controller has his own muttering style: some like to pace, some like to sit quietly and some are fast and fluent, while others are constantly clicking back to record over a sentence they've changed their mind about. It's a very public exercise and I confess that I write my first memo out secretly by hand to conceal how much time I've spent on it before dictating it from memory – or rather, *performing* it in the open plan office – fluently and with what I perceive to be a certain commercial élan into my lovely new silver Dictaphone. Disappointingly, nobody pays me any attention. I think about waiting for some of the other controllers to return to their desks and doing a repeat performance but decide against it on the grounds that if somebody *was* actually listening first time around I'll just look deeply sad.

File memos are the red blood cells of the office, each one freshly generated by a controller to carry a little story around the office and transport it to the appropriate cabinet for filing. Each memo is printed out in three colours: a blue one (top copy for the recipient), a green one (for the file, so it can be located easily in a thick file of documents) and a pink one (collected into a weekly pack known as 'the Pinks', which rather sounds like a 1960s pop group) which is circulated to everyone in the office 'for information'. Actually the real purpose of the Pinks is as a means of attracting the attention of – and impressing – your colleagues, particularly your boss. It's a little moment of pathetically smug satisfaction when the Pinks come around a day or so later and I see a scrawled note from Cicero, in blue fountain pen ink, on my first ever memo:

Paul, good note!
C.

The truth is that I enjoyed writing the note more than I enjoyed the meeting itself. The note became an act of alchemy by which I transformed an unremarkable, meandering and fruitless conversation into a crisp, commercially meaningful encounter.

I especially liked the bit about a 'Tier 2' automotive supplier. That wasn't actually mentioned at all during the meeting; it was just something I picked up from chat around the office. But it adds a veneer of sophistication, don't you think?

November 1985

I'm finding my feet and get to look at my first proper business plan.

Dabble and I get called through to the front office to see Clump, who hands him a business plan that has come in the post. It's also a good opportunity to give 'young Traynor' some early experience of a real deal. I think that's almost the first time he's acknowledged my existence. He asks to be 'kept in the loop' and then picks up his phone and starts to dial. We're clearly dismissed.

As we cross the corridor back to our desks I can tell Dabble wants to say 'tosser' or some such thing, but he restrains himself. He gives me the business plan and tells me to read it, making some dismissive remark that if it's come in the post the chances are it will be crap.

Well, I read it and I don't think it's crap. Everything I've been shown to date has been scrappy financial statements, sometimes even handwritten, but this is a proper business plan. It's neatly printed and someone has even taken the trouble to bind all the pages together. And when I turn the pages I'm blown away by how much information it contains: a really good description of the business, a concise summary of what investment they need and why, and a whole section of comprehensive financial information including detailed three-year forecasts. There's even an executive summary. It occurs to me that I could copy most of it straight across into a Submission. It's all so thorough and professional and seems to cover not only everything I need to know, but lots of things I hadn't even thought of as well. I honestly can't imagine why we even need a meeting; personally I'd be happy to send them a cheque in the post. For the first time, I feel the seductive tug of a well-presented case.

Dabble doesn't really like travelling out to visit the company on a first meeting; it's very inefficient in his view. So the managing director is summoned to us and we meet him in the cramped little meeting room behind reception. He's the third generation of his family to run the business and he's local and sensible, although not particularly sophisticated. He's brought a sample book of carpet tiles, which he hands over. Dabble flicks through them with that lemon-sour look of disapproval on his face. You'd think he was being asked to buy some for his living room.

The MD is clearly picking up this sense of disdain as he sets off on a long-winded explanation about the essential properties of *commercial* carpets, as opposed to *retail* ones. Dabble responds by picking up one tile by the corner, holding it pretty much at arm's length and giving it the eye, like it's a snotty handker-chief or a used nappy. The MD wants to illustrate his point by reference to the tile that Dabble is holding, so he reaches across to take it back. But Dabble resists and for a moment or two it looks like an unseemly tug of war is about to start over a commercial carpet tile.

At this point the door opens to reveal Alex, carrying a tray of tea and coffee. Because she needs both hands to carry the tray, she's had to kick the door hard and it slams back against the stops.

'Whoops,' she giggles.

She sways around the large table, searching for a spot to deposit the tray. This involves bending forward; her top tightens, and I realise the MD has suspended his monologue mid-word, an expression on his face like a tortured rabbit staring at two headlights.

Alex pirouettes away, giggles again – why, I'm not quite sure – and bumps the door with her hip on the way out to dislodge it. It swings shut behind her, stirring up the air and giving us a momentary waft of her lingering perfume.

Dabble is still holding the floor tile between pinched finger and thumb, regarding it distastefully. He hasn't even looked up. The MD's eyes meet mine and he seems to want to say something but needs to wait as his Adam's apple is shooting up and down like a frenzied lift in an elevator shaft. Eventually he gets it under control enough to speak.

'Fucking hell!' he says.

I start using the word *upside* a lot, even though I'm still not entirely sure what it means. There's a whole new vocabulary to learn and use and, even if I don't quite understand it all, it just makes me sound so *commercial*. I never say 'directors' or 'the board' or 'the entrepreneur' anymore – I just say 'management' instead. I don't talk about shares or shareholdings either – I just say 'equity'. It's all so cool.

In order to win deals we have to be good at 'selling', apparently. There's a 'selling' course that forms part of our training but I'm not scheduled to take it for several months at least. In the meantime, it's a question of observing the others and learning. I go out to various meetings with Callum, Salty and Bunny but can't even work out when they are actually 'selling'. The meetings seem to follow a standard pattern. It begins with asking the MD to 'tell us about the business in his own words.' He then rambles on for some time with the controller trying, usually with limited success, to intervene and keep him on track. It's like watching someone chase a chicken around a yard: just when you think they've nailed him down to a particular question, like how much profit the company actually made last year, the chicken squawks and heads off sharply in another direction. Since the most common characteristic amongst those who manage small enterprises seems to be an infinite capacity for garrulous irrelevance, I would have thought courses on 'interrupting' or 'developing the patience of a frigging saint' would be far more useful than one on 'selling'.

I do go to a couple of meetings where we actually make an offer, which involves presenting an offer letter on headed 3i notepaper, which runs to a lot of pages. It's very legalistic, with plenty of numbered paragraphs and *hereinafter referred to*s and *notwithstanding*s, and 'selling' seems to involve nothing more than taking the management painstakingly through the clauses, explaining the meaning of each one and handling any objections or clarifications. If the manager survives to the end of this process, he is invited to countersign the letter. If this is 'selling' then it seems to me that selling is pretty boring.

Bunny invites me to a meeting to present some terms to a management team. It's a relatively big deal so he invites Clump along to add some gravitas – or, more likely, Clump invites himself. Bunny has a stack of offer letters and puts them down on the desk, presumably planning to circulate them, but Clump just takes over, skidding copies across the desk to the three managers. I don't think he's actually met this team before but he spends the first five minutes bombarding them with compliments, enthusing effusively about the investment opportunity, telling them that he's been following them for years and this is the most exciting thing he's seen in a long time. He tells them 3i is only asking for 35% of the equity, which is a fantastic deal. So much so, in fact, that he's not even certain the number isn't a typo: personally he would have demanded at least 60%. Either way the terms are ridiculously attractive so his advice to the management team is to sign up quickly before 3i changes its mind. Or spots the typo.

Management are helpless before this tsunami of chutzpah, flattery and misdirection. Clump has even brought extra pens for them to sign with. They sign up, there are handshakes all round and everyone parts the best of friends.

Well, whatever that was, it certainly wasn't boring. It felt very uncomfortable though, like watching a cheesy car salesman talk a young mother of four into buying a two-seater convertible sports car for the school run. I feel a bit sorry for Bunny as well, who was completely erased as a presence in the meeting. He makes a bit of a joke about it to me afterwards, when Clump's out of earshot, but it feels a bit forced. I think if somebody stole a meeting off me like that I'd be crushed.

I'm sitting on a packing case in an office in an industrial unit just off St Paul's Square. The managing director is sitting at his desk and Callum has the only other chair in the room. Which leaves me on the packing case.

The meeting has come about as a result of a cold call and, despite having been there for twenty minutes, we still haven't found out what the business actually does. Callum has asked three times now, in slightly different ways, but the MD has managed to monologue extensively without even flirting with the possibility of enlightening us. He also has the habit – which I am beginning to discover is maddeningly typical amongst MDs – of answering his telephone mid-flow, dealing with the caller, then resuming his meaningless rant, usually from a different point to where he left off. The problem is that since *we've* asked for the meeting, we're kind of under an obligation to put up with it. My mind drifts. It's cold in the room and my backside is hurting. My feet don't quite touch the floor and I'm struggling to suppress the urge to swing them like a schoolboy sitting on a garden wall.

Something pricks my attention and I retune into the monologue. The MD is blasting 'those greedy bastards from ICFC who take equity in your company.' This is interesting because we *are* ICFC. Or at least we were, until about two years ago when we changed our name to Investors in Industry – 3i.

Awkward. I wonder how Callum is going to deal with this one.

'Yeah,' he agrees, 'ICFC are bastards.'

I've progressed to the point where I am handling most of the telephone GEs that are coming in. Or perhaps it's more accurate to say that, when the girls phone up from reception saying there's a GE on the phone, everybody but me disappears for a toilet break or is suddenly very, very busy. I don't mind though. It's actually quite fun to joust with the caller, see what information you can extract and then try to bounce them without provoking an argument. I'm not actually expecting any deals to materialise though. I'm the waiter tidying away all the plates with unwanted food on them.

I take a telephone GE from a terribly polite gentleman who informs me that he enjoys spending time watching the planes at Birmingham Airport. Since his retirement he and the wife have rather got into the habit, several times a week, of making up a picnic box, filling their vacuum flask with hot sweet coffee and spending the day in the long-stay car park under the runway flight path. As a retirement gift, his wife bought him a most miraculous pair of Zeiss binoculars which have enabled him to watch the ground operations in hitherto unimaginable detail.

He's noticed that the luggage bins that are loaded into the aircraft have small wooden pallets, and it's occurred to him that he could easily knock up one or two of those in his garden shed for next to nothing. Since he's not terribly busy these days, he is thinking that here is an opportunity for him to supplement his modest retirement income by making a few pallets and selling them to the airlines. He's read about Investors in Industry and the marvellous work we do in supporting start-ups. Would we be interested in supporting his business venture?

I ask him how much he's looking to raise and he says he hasn't 'done his homework' yet but just wanted to discuss the idea in principle before committing too much time to the project.

I suggest that he would need to put a business plan together which, amongst other things, specifies the amount of funding he would need. He says this feedback is immensely helpful and compliments me on the professional way in which I have handled the discussion.

As I put the telephone back in its cradle, I realise my defences were dulled by his deference and I've broken the first rule of bouncing: never to set a hurdle for the caller to clear.

Unlikely he'll be back, though.

December 1985

I attend my first business lunch.

It's held in our boardroom, which has a large black table that can accommodate twenty people at a pinch. We've hired some caterers who produce a full three-course hot meal from somewhere – is there a kitchen on the premises? The waiting staff are all formidably built ladies of a certain age, dressed in black with white aprons, and they all speak fluent Brummie.

There are about eight invitees, comprising two of our favourite advisers (one lawyer and one accountant, to avoid professional jealousy), three 'target companies' (MDs of companies we would like to invest in if we get the opportunity) and three existing customers. Cicero hosts, supported by Clump, one controller from the New Business Team and one from the Portfolio Team. And me.

No one explains it to me but I gather the purpose of the event is to impress the invitees sufficiently enough that they will want to do business with us. So the advisers are there to be impressed by the quality of the companies we know, the message being that we can potentially introduce a lot of great new clients to you – if, of course, you do the same for us. This exchange of commercial favours even has a name: patronage, which sounds a bit feudal, or possibly like a method for selecting archbishops. The target companies are there to be impressed with the quality of the existing customers, so much so that they want to become one. They're also supposed to be impressed by the quality of advisers that we could introduce them to. I'm less sure what the existing customers are doing here. Maybe they just need a bit of company. Everyone says that managing a small business is a lonely endeavour.

I'm no marketing expert, but it strikes me as a bit strange that nobody actually mentions the purpose of the lunch. In fact, if I didn't know better, I'd say that everyone is going out of their way to *avoid* acknowledging what we are all really doing here. Instead, we have lots of business small talk. Business small talk, it turns out, is even duller and more interminable than social small talk. Everybody asks everybody else if they are busy. And, yes, it seems that everybody is indeed busy. Very busy. Never been busier. Then we have lots of name dropping, except that it's a specialised elite form of name dropping that eliminates the need for surnames. Cicero mentions that he's just had a meeting with *Derek* who recently bumped into *Geoff*, who is also very busy. One of the advisers is prompted by this remark to say that he also saw *Geoff* recently, which in turn reminded him of how much he admires what *Steve* – who he hasn't seen for a while – did with the business. Someone else chips in that *Martin* was looking terribly well last week, while another congratulates *Philip* on his recent success. I'm utterly lost. It's like being at a gathering of film critics when you haven't seen the films. Who the fuck is Geoff and WTF did Steve do with his business that deserves our unconditional admiration?

As dessert is being served, Cicero raps his spoon on his

wineglass and does a little speech, welcoming everyone. Here we go, I think, this is the part where we ask if anyone has a deal we could look at. Instead, Cicero throws out a general question about the state of the economy and wonders what the prospects are of an imminent recession. Clump interjects to make a playful joke about the 3i Investment Committee having forecast ten out of the last two recessions. I've only been in the company a couple of weeks and I've heard him use this quip about five times already. It's rather lost on the non-3i contingent though. Nevertheless, the invitees pick up on Cicero's initiative and all make speeches about the economic situation, with plenty of homespun advice for the Chancellor of the Exchequer. Sadly the government didn't think to send anyone along to hear how very straightforward it is to sort out the country's appalling economic malaise. One particularly corpulent MD has evidently placed himself on a diet because he is trying to refuse a very sugary-looking dessert whilst simultaneously holding forth about the scandal of the Sterling-Deutschmark exchange rate. For some reason, the serving lady isn't taking no for an answer and he has to flap his hand like a picnicker trying to rid himself of a troublesome wasp. She's not one for giving up though and we all become silently absorbed by this tussle, which frankly is a lot more interesting than his views on the UK government's economic incompetency. The situation only resolves itself when she forcibly wedges her considerable bulk between him and the next guest, enabling her to slop a large portion of what I think is Eton Mess triumphantly down onto his vacant plate.

'Thur yow go luvvie!' she cackles. Then, perhaps prompted into an explanation by the sudden silence in the room, she adds 'Yow luke like yow enjoy yow food.'

One–nil to the serving lady. The good news for us is that Mr

Corpulent completely loses his thread and, before he can reboot his dreary monologue, somebody else jumps in and takes over the conversation.

We get to the end of the event without any exploration whatsoever of mutual business opportunities. Clearly marketing is a more subtle and mysterious business than I had appreciated.

Birmingham is a strange place. The city centre is a big knot of shops and offices squeezed in a permanent chokehold by a stained concrete octopus of subterranean roads, ramps, tunnels and pedestrian subways into which you descend at peril of never finding your way back out again. The Bull Ring looks like some junior urban planner's botched homework project abandoned on top of New Street Station. After a couple of weeks in my executive single room at the Holiday Inn, I venture out into the city to look for somewhere to buy or rent. Most of the suburbs are featureless, characterless and rather look as though they have been constructed entirely out of Formica, Linoleum and PVC window frames. Moseley has a sort of shabby chicness about it that reminds me of Hackney. Sutton Coldfield is one of those areas that estate agents like to describe as 'sought after' but it's a bit solidly middle-class for me, and it would be a struggle to drive to work every morning traversing the M6 at Spaghetti junction and bumping and grinding down the clogged A38(M).

South of the city centre, I discover an oasis in the form of the Bournville village estate, a twee picture-postcard model village originally built by the Cadburys for their workers and where, standing in the open air, you can catch the scent of roasting cocoa beans from the chocolate factory. I fall instantly in love with a tiny cottage for sale there; to my surprise, I discover I can actually afford it and put in an offer, which is accepted. The house purchase will take some time to go through so, in the meantime, I rent a modern two-bedroom flat in the supposedly upmarket area of Edgbaston. The flat itself is in a two-storey block surrounded by a manicured lawn. There are lots of these blocks in Edgbaston. They look like rectangular birthday cakes, decorated with uPVC icing and plonked on a green marzipan base. From the air it must seem like a colony of property developers arranged a joint birthday party to which they all forgot to turn up. To get to the office in the mornings I have to drive along Broad Street, which is a mile of little more than rubble and derelict buildings.

One evening there is an office outing to Stoney Lane in Balsall Heath, where it seems several of the houses have turned their front rooms into eating places (restaurants would be far too sophisticated a word for them). We sit at a plastic table, and everything on the menu is curry served with luscious thick breads that you use instead of cutlery. I honestly don't believe I've tasted anything so good in all my life.

The polite gentleman with the airport proposal calls me up to let me know he's making excellent progress putting his business plan together. In particular the municipal library in Birmingham city centre is proving to be a most useful research facility. He has nothing further to report at this particular time but thought he would just give me a call to 'keep me in the loop' as no doubt I was wondering how he was getting on.

Despite the absence of any obvious rapport between Dabble and the MD of the commercial floor-tiling company, Dabble has decided to open a case file. This means he is serious about trying to do a deal.

There is a big green book in the office that is used to allocate a case number when a case is opened. Each page is divided into columns, which are filled in by hand, starting with the first column where you write in the next case number in sequence, then the company name, then the purpose of the investment and finally the amount requested.

It's a rollcall of every deal ever done by 3i Birmingham and contains the autograph of pretty much every controller who has worked there since the office opened in 1950. It feels more like a manuscript recovered from an ancient monastery than a management record. I actually feel quite solemn opening the book and writing in the details of Dabble's new case against the next serial number, including the amount: £250,000.

This means that, when the weekly WIP sheet is produced, the case moves out of GEs into the 'opened' category, which gives Dabble his little peacock moment at the next Monday meeting.

He explains that we are now waiting for an industrial adviser's report, which is likely to take three to four weeks. Industrial advisers are ex-businessmen employed by 3i to visit the companies we propose to invest in. They write a report that is attached to the Submission when it goes to whoever needs to approve it. The industrial adviser concludes each report by saying whether the proposed investment is supported or not supported. If he doesn't support it you basically have no chance of getting it approved.

Industrial advisers work out of our Solihull administrative office. They're all useless tossers and our implacable enemies.

Apparently.

In the meantime Dabble suggests I start putting together the Submission. Jo prints off a blank Submission template from the Wang and gives it to me to handwrite onto. After I've put on the name and address of the company, the names of the directors and their shareholdings, I get temporarily stuck on the SIC code. Is it *13931 Manufacture of woven or tufted carpets and rugs* or *13939 Manufacture of other carpets and rugs*? In the end I plump for the second one, gambling that nobody really gives a flying fuck.

Now I'm onto the 'Scheme' section, which is where you summarise the terms of the investment proposal. I've seen enough Submissions now to improvise and put in what I understand to be the standard scheme. We'll provide most of the £250,000 investment by way of a loan repayable over fifteen years – which is an enormously long time in financial terms. Most banks won't do more than three to five years. Our loan will be secured by a debenture, which is to say that if the company goes bust we get to appoint a receiver to sell the assets of the business and, if he succeeds in getting anything for them, the proceeds will be used to reduce our losses. We charge eye-watering rates of interest, probably about 12%, although we only make a margin of 2.5% on that. This is 1985 and Bank Base Rates are about 9%.

The commercial proposition is quite simple. With the benefit of the extra cash, the company grows its profits, enabling it to pay our interest and repay our loan whilst also increasing the dividends to shareholders and, ultimately, the value of the company. We get a healthy income by way of interest and we gradually recover our money so that eventually (after fifteen years in this case) our capital will have been fully repaid. Because we're taking a risk – if the company goes bust we will probably lose some if not all of our investment – we also take a share of the equity, and benefit from the dividends and from the increase in the value of the company. So the company gets its growth capital, we get some interest and the bulk of our money back in time and are left with a potentially very valuable investment that we'll turn into cash if and when the company is sold.

It's a win-win deal.

Except that owner-managers think it's a total rip off. We think we're taking appropriate compensation for the risks we're taking. They think that we're just greedy bastards. Entrepreneurs think that surrendering a share of their company just to obtain a loan is about as reasonable as Rumpelstiltskin demanding your daughter just for converting a bit of straw into gold. There is usually outrage, often spectacularly so, when we first propose this exchange. In anticipating it, controllers have been known to melt down, babble or say the exact opposite of what they mean. We call this 'hitting the equity panic button'. Senior controllers like to brighten up an otherwise dull day by getting a trainee to present an offer letter, specifically for the entertainment value in watching the poor soul hit the equity panic button and get into a total tangle when the entrepreneur roars fire and fury at them.

I'm not sure how to work out how much of the equity we should ask for, and since I suspect I'll be the one hitting the equity panic button here, I don't want to make my job even harder by putting in too big a number. I leave that bit blank, making a note to ask Dabble later. But that's all in the future anyway as we won't be making a proposal to management until the industrial adviser's report is back and the Submission is formally approved by Cicero. For the moment I'm insulated from such stressful decisions and it's just a question of practicing my Submission writing. There's a long section where you're supposed to describe the business, the management and the deal, but I decide to leave that until later and move on to the financial section. It's a simple matter of transcribing the accounts in the business plan into the standard 3i format: profit & loss statement, balance sheet and funds flow, followed by the interest, capital repayments and dividends arising from our investment.

Well, it should be simple. It's only when I start to transcribe the numbers that I realise all the categories are slightly different. The business plan has 'gross profit' whereas we use 'contribution', which is something else. When I try to make the necessary adjustments, the numbers go all weird, the balance sheet doesn't balance and the cashflow goes ballistic.

I'm determined not to ask for help. How hard can this be?

Quite hard, actually. I take it home at the weekend and spend most of Sunday trying all sorts of arithmetical manipulations to get the figures to balance, getting more and more frustrated. Finally, late on Sunday afternoon, it suddenly clicks into place. In an instant the volcano of frustration inside me subsides and is replaced with the sort of calm contentment that I've previously only seen on the face of my two-year-old nephew when he's finally released into his nappy the thing that's been bothering him for days.

I take a telephone call from a man with a very strong Brummie accent. He asks me if I have ever used a jasookoi?

A what?

It sounds vaguely Japanese – perhaps it's a make of car, or the latest fad for kids? No, it's a system of pumps that blow bubbles in your bath. The penny drops.

'Oh, you mean a jacuzzi?'

'Yur, roight, a jasookoi.'

It turns out the caller is a plumber who has just encountered his first jacuzzi and found it inspirational. He asks me if I know how many homes have showers today compared to ten years ago? I feel we're jumping around a little but go with it.

'Don't know, how many?'

'Lowds,' he states, smugly.

To be honest, I was expecting something a little more statistically substantial but I get his drift. He is claiming that jacuzzies are the next big thing in bathroom fashion and, within ten years, there will be one in pretty much every house. I can't say I'm immediately convinced.

The caller runs a one-man plumbing business in the affluent suburb of Solihull, which is where he met his first jasookoi. Impulsively, he's already ordered a container load from Italy which is due to arrive in three weeks' time. Unfortunately, he doesn't have the money to pay for the delivery and is now in a panic. He's talked to his bank but they've refused to increase his overdraft or give him a loan and suggested he gives 3i a call. So he wants to borrow some money. He reckons he can probably install at least a couple of jasookois a week and should be able to pay us back within a few weeks of the container arriving. I ask how much he's having to pay for the delivery.

'£5,000.'

I say no because the amount is below our minimum investment threshold.

He tells me to fuck off and the line goes dead.

Assessing managers and management teams is a big part of the job and there's always a discussion about how good the team is. Nobody really *teaches* you what to look for in a manager, but there's a distinctive vocabulary that gets used so it's a question of picking up the phrases and matching them with people you meet. Good managing directors should be *dynamic, driven* and possess *a good eye for detail,* while finance directors should be *tough, conservative* and *focused on cost control.* There are also different categories of manager: proprietorial ones (unambitious, uneducated, not backable) and professional ones (urbane, ambitious, very backable). There's also a third, very exciting, category I've heard talked about but haven't met yet– or at least haven't been aware of meeting: the entrepreneur.

So, it's some considerable curiosity and even a little excitement that I experience when Clump bustles into the office and tells me to get my jacket on. He's got a treat for me. It's an opportunity to meet a 'real entrepreneur'. The treat turns out to be that I'm accompanying him to a meeting in Henley-in-Arden, where all the truly stinking rich of Birmingham live, to meet this 'real entrepreneur'. As we drive there I'm left in no doubt that this guy is a serious player and that Clump is very, very close to him.

Our destination is a townhouse right in the centre of Henley, a quaint Warwickshire town with mock-Tudor houses, cream tea restaurants and designer fabric shops. From the outside, the address looks like the sort of place that is often converted into a dentist's surgery or an office for a small local firm of solicitors. But, after being greeted at the door by an attractive but overly made-up young woman, we are shown into an office that has purple walls, an enormous black leather sofa, a white shagpile carpet, a marble coffee table and a huge fish tank, from which various tropical fish mouth mindlessly at me. It's like the set of a 1970s porn movie. If I had been bold enough to watch *Lezzes in Latex* at the Hyde Park hotel I have a feeling I might well have recognised this as the location. There's no table so I have to sit on the sofa – rather fearful of what I might be sitting in – right next to Clump. It all feels very uncomfortable.

The 'entrepreneur' must be in his sixties, with a face so lined by prolonged exposure to the sun that it looks like a baked mudflat. He doesn't wear a suit, his shirt is open by at least two unnecessary buttons and his thinning, grey hair is tied back in a ponytail. As far as I can work out, his thing is to acquire 'interests' which he then merges with other 'interests'. This process of reshuffling deckchairs mysteriously converts a small pile of money into a much larger one. In fact, he's now sitting on such a large pile of cash that he risks being seriously embarrassed with the Inland Revenue. Accordingly he has recently acquired a shell[3] company for its accumulated tax losses and now wants to flip this into a listed company alongside some of his 'interests', thereby massively reducing his tax liability. To facilitate this he's looking for an investor for 'fifty mill' who will, he assures us, be able to double his money within six months. I have no idea what *flipping* is but it sounds a frighteningly casual thing to do with fifty million pounds. Does 3i do *flipping*? Is there any commercial purpose to *flipping* other than to bamboozle the taxman? Is it even legal? Ethical? How does 3i feel about being associated with tossing large sums of money out of the pan just to strip them of their tax liability? And would we ever

---

3 A company which has made such horrendous losses that it had to shut down. Rather than liquidate the company, however, at this time tax legislation allowed the shareholders to sell on the empty shell to another company which could then apply the historic losses to their current profits.

provide a £50m pancake anyway? Sure, we have a £3bn balance sheet, but the biggest deal I've ever seen us do is £1m and the average is much lower than that. I've witnessed some thoroughly bonkers GEs already but this one is surely grandiosely wacky. Nonetheless, Clump gushes enthusiastically and says that he'll 'talk it through with our CEO and get a feel for our position.' I raise my eyebrows at this. I wasn't aware that our CEO was available to discuss breaking investment opportunities. There are over twenty UK offices and several more abroad – if our CEO is making himself available to chat through new GEs then I doubt he's going to have time to do much CEOing, whatever that entails. The way Clump is talking puts me in mind of an excitable puppy desperate to deposit the colourful bird between its teeth at the feet of its applauding master.

I thought entrepreneurs were visionaries, creators of things, forceful personalities. Mudflat just comes across as a dodgy dealer who has somehow contrived to become wealthy. Clump, however, seems starstruck and talks admiringly about him all the way back to the office. I'm confused. Is my radar so badly off?

We get back to the office and my problem now is that I have to write the file memo. I have no idea what the business actually does and my firm impression is that the entrepreneur is about as backable as Del Boy Trotter. But I'm pretty sure Clump is expecting a somewhat more positive account when it appears in the Pinks. I take myself and my silver Dictaphone off to a secluded meeting room and put on my finest creative writing hat.

'This is an opportunity to participate in a complex and sophisticated corporate restructuring project involving a highly profitable group of well-established businesses ...'

I don't, in point of fact, have any numbers to back up the notion that the businesses are *highly profitable*. Or even profitable at all. But let's take that as read for the moment. After all, I don't know that they're *not* profitable. The weird thing is how that sentence starts to make the thing sound really rather compelling ...

'Our meeting was with the chairman – a locally well-respected and vastly experienced entrepreneur – who is clearly the driving force behind the group and the architect of the proposed reconstruction. Highly numerate with a sharp commercial edge, his achievements seem to have been grounded on a shrewd eye for an acquisition and a commendable ability to delegate effectively the day-to-day management of the group to capable managers of the operational subsidiaries ...'

Bloody hell! I'm beginning to want to back the guy myself.

I hand the tape to Alex for typing and she tells me that Clump scurried off alone to a meeting room as I was dictating the memo, but she has no idea who he called or if he even made a call. Later, when I venture an enquiry as to how it went, he changes the subject and the meeting with Mudflat is never mentioned again.

I keep an eye on the newspapers but never see any evidence that someone else successfully pulled off any 'fifty mill' flipping. Or went to jail trying.

Curiously, when the Pinks next come around there's no sign of my carefully crafted memo to file. Alex must have forgotten to circulate it.

There's an avalanche of completions in December, something to do with everybody wanting to get the deal done by the calendar year end – or just so they can enjoy Christmas. Callum has about three deals due to complete, and Bunny and Salty a couple each, while Dabble is hoping to get a positive report on Latham

Flooring from the industrial adviser and rush the legals through before Christmas. Having been lagging behind the office cash out target for the year, it's now looking like we'll be well ahead of budget by Christmas. The other controllers are good about letting me help out on their deals but it's not the same as doing one yourself. I feel like there's a party going on and I'm outside looking in through the window. I'm getting an almost physical ache to get a deal under my belt from start to finish.

The industrial adviser's report on Latham finally arrives the week before Christmas, but it's *'Not Supported'*. Dabble is not happy. I'm just astonished. The business plan was so seductive.

The Adviser Report contains a two-page summary and then an expanded explanation, running to perhaps eight pages of prose and some numbers at the back. Obviously by the time I get to read it I already know what the conclusion is, whilst nevertheless bearing in mind that all industrial advisers are tossers. What I learn is that, in essence, the adviser appreciates that the company has many good points but, all the same, it's operating in a highly competitive market and this, in his view, is likely to put downward pressure on prices and make finding new customers challenging. In short, he thinks it's unlikely the business will achieve the forecasts in the business plan. Dabble speaks to him on the phone and has a bit of a rant but, although I obviously don't say so, if I was forced to choose I would side with the adviser. What he writes is so utterly reasonable, informed and *persuasive*. After he's put the phone down, Dabble calls him a prat. But the deal's as dead as a dodo. At the last Monday morning WIP meeting before Christmas, poor Dabble has to sit through a reading of all the deals being completed by the others and then draw everyone's attention to the fact that Latham Flooring, his only deal, has moved from 'Opened' to

'Rejected'. Cicero is supportive and tidies the problem quickly away with his hands but Clump snorts, tuts, rolls his eyes and makes some disparaging remarks. He's being a bit of a bastard to be honest, and Dabble tries to look like it's water off a duck's back, but he doesn't really manage it. I feel sorry for him.

My problem is a different one. As I read the report I get this emptying feeling inside; what the adviser says seems so *obvious*, except that it wasn't obvious to me at all when I read the business plan or met the guy. The investment looked totally sound to me and, left to my own devices, I would have cheerfully and unhesitatingly lent them the money.

Am I ever going to be any good at this?

The office Christmas party is outrageous. Within half an hour we're already merry and in very high spirits. There's a meal, party hats and drinking games. Boys are pitted against girls and the winners have to exchange clothes for the rest of the lunch.

At some point during the afternoon, when things have become very fuzzy, I encounter Alex on the stairs. She pushes me against the wall and gives me a deep wet snog full on the lips. Then she laughs and dances away. It's a strange and wonderful moment for many reasons, one of which is that she's dressed in Cicero's pinstripe suit.

Well, I'm pretty sure it was Alex.

Christmas Eve is very quiet. I open up the mail and discover I have received a Christmas card from Airport Man. In neat handwriting – he's even used a fountain pen – he wishes me a *Very Merry Yuletide and a Happy New Year.* There is a footnote to say that he continues to make excellent progress on his business plan, which he expects to be in a position to share with me early in the New Year.

We finish officially at 2 p.m. and it feels a bit strange to be driving down to London. I won't be back now until the New Year. It's been a fascinating couple of months, even though I haven't made sense of a lot of it. I do feel at home in a way I never did at my previous job. On the other hand, I'm becoming almost painfully desperate to take my place amongst the ranks by actually doing a deal and I'm hoping things are going to really kick on in January. I'm still a trainee for another fifteen months but I've seen that nobody holds anyone back in this place. I'm nominally still attached to Dabble but I'm already growing in independence. If a decent opportunity comes in, I'm more than ready to have a crack at it myself.

Just before I leave, the telephone rings – it's a GE. The caller explains that he manages a family company just around the corner from us which has been doing particularly well in the run-up to Christmas. They need an injection of working capital and the bank has steered them in our direction. Unusually, the caller sounds eminently sensible and answers all my questions concisely. What's more, the project seems to fit squarely within our investment criteria. The caller confirms he has a business plan that he could send to me and I say absolutely, yes please. I'll take a look at it and respond first thing in the New Year.

I make a note of the company name: Samji Industries Limited. It's the first telephone GE I've taken that sounds half-promising.

4

THE TRAINING BUDGET

'Fools, as it has long been said, are indeed separated, soon
or eventually, from their money. So, alas, are those who,
responding to a general mood of optimism, are captured
by a sense of their own financial acumen.'

J K Galbraith

January 1986

Before we start back at the office, there's a big trip to London
for the whole team, both controllers and secretaries. 3i holds an
annual New Year's party for the whole company, a lavish and
extravagant affair held at the Grosvenor Hotel in Park Lane.
There must be five or six hundred people there, including support
staff, and we're put up – all at the company's expense – in the
Tower Bridge Hotel.

There are a few speeches, an awful lot of which seem to
involve jokes about Scottish people. Apparently the company
is riddled with them.

Later, back at the hotel, a group of us move from room to

room systematically emptying the minibars. Every time we emerge from one room in order to move to the next, a very loud Scotsman charges past us in the corridor pushing a supermarket trolley with a different girl in it.

For internal 3i use only

3i MEMORANDUM

From: **Paul Traynor**
To: **File**
Date: **9th January 1986**
Subject: **Samji Industries Limited**

Following a telephone call from the de facto managing director, Deepak Samji, I visited the company on 8th January. This is a growth capital opportunity.

The company, which operates from a small rented workshop just off the Bristol Road, assembles wooden and plastic frames for posters and paintings. The product is sold to independent retailers, who usually combine the frame with a picture or poster rather than selling it on in its own right. For the retailer, the cost of the frame is an important consideration but variety (both in terms of style and size) is also important. Samji has built up a network of 50+ independent retailers who like and trust the product and, accordingly, now source exclusively from the company.

The company has grown rapidly in the last few years. Last audited accounts, for the year to December 1984 show sales of £643k (net profit £57k) but management accounts for the year just closed (December 1985) show a sharp increase to £983k (net profit £91k). Management have produced a three-year forecast which anticipates revenues growing to £1.35m, at which point the company expects to be generating a net profit (before interest) of £175k. The company is funded by means of a £50k overdraft facility from Lloyds bank, secured primarily by a charge on stock and debtors. There are no other borrowings.

The company is owned by Samji Senior, who started the business on moving to the UK about 15 years ago. However the company has only really started to grow since his eldest son, Deepak (age 29) took over as de facto managing director. Deepak is a driven and commercial individual who spotted the opportunity to establish the business in the independent retailer base. In addition to Deepak, there are three other sons, all of whom work in the business covering sales, warehouse and back office respectively. They come across as a dynamic and harmonious team, but are also ambitious for the business. Samji Senior has little active involvement in the business these days, although he retains the title of chairman and managing director. If we were to invest it would have to be conditional on the titles and equity reflecting more accurately the real, as opposed to the ceremonial, roles of the various members of the family. There is no doubt that the company would also benefit from the involvement of an experienced non-executive chairman, which is something that they would welcome.

The current network of independent retailers is largely restricted to the West Midlands area, which means there is an obvious opportunity for geographical expansion. This growth trend is already well established and placing some strain on the company's overdraft. Management have approached us with a request for funding of £125k for working capital and to provide a degree of contingency.

> Although the company is small at present, I was impressed by the ambition and drive of the young team and the prospects for the company are potentially quite exciting. In discussing the role 3i could play in supporting the company's growth plans, it was clear that the team were attracted by 3i's long term, hands-off approach.

Samji Industries is located just off the Bristol Road and within easy walking distance of the 3i office. The door, solid enough to smother the incessant groaning of heavily-laden lorries toiling up the A38 outside, has not seen a fresh coat of paint in decades and is battered with locks and bolts to keep out the late-night drunks from the Dome nightclub next door. I am greeted by Deepak Samji who is a sensible, pleasant lad in his late twenties (and therefore a few years older than me) and the person I spoke to on the telephone just before Christmas. Deepak introduces me to his father, Samji Senior, who occupies an office partitioned away from the hubbub of workshop activity, with his title on the door. It is as if he has been filed away under 'Chairman and Managing Director' in case anyone should ever wish to take him out and look him up. Samji Senior shakes my hand a little too effusively, both of his hands over mine, and gestures for me to take the rickety plastic chair opposite him. Although the office itself overflows with box files and folders, from which ill-disciplined documents half-spill, his desk – in cheap pine from some knock-off shop in Moseley or Willenhall – is uncluttered except for a bruised green plastic telephone, a pristine notepad and one freshly-sharpened HB pencil. Our conversation is brief, stilted, awkward and requires frequent interventions from Deepak to translate.

The formalities of introduction complete, Deepak gives me a tour of the workshop. There are perhaps twenty-five or thirty staff, all of Indian origin, distributed around several crowded workbenches and all busy snapping together basic picture frames and fixing them in place with hand-held staple guns. There's a comforting air of bustle about the place. Deepak explains that the business needs more stock and more workers to keep up with growing demand: £125,000 should be more than enough, he thinks. He takes me to his office, smaller than that of his father, and shows me the accounts. He explains that his father set up the company a number of years ago and still owns all the shares, but it is effectively now run by himself and his younger brothers. I find myself liking Deepak and warming to him. Moreover, the numbers in the accounts make sense and it dawns on me that I've not yet encountered any reason why we shouldn't do this – a slightly disorientating but rather thrilling feeling. Unsure of my ground, however, I am careful not to make any promises before I leave, except that I will think about it and get back to Deepak within a few days.

I am discovering that I have quite a talent for writing memos. Like most of the meetings I have been to so far, the encounter with the Samjis was fragmentary, incomplete and unsatisfactory. In a file memo, it becomes organised, purposeful and commercial.

It's all about the skilful recycling of words, phrases and the clichés I have been absorbing from my fellow controllers faster than spilled ink on a blotting pad. You need to show that you've mastered the detail but retain a comprehensive overview. It's always good to describe management as *impressive* and *ambitious*. The word *opportunity* should be sprinkled delicately over the memo – like just the right amount of salt on a dish – to set an optimistic tone and it's always good to imply that management really like and respect 3i. It's also a good idea to mention an 'issue' – the need for a non-executive director or chairman is always a good one – to show that you're not being moon-eyed about the investment.

Actually, the bit in the memo about the non-executive chairman isn't *quite* accurate. I meant to raise that at the meeting but completely forgot. However, I'm sure that's what they *would* have said if I *had* remembered to mention it.

Anyway the proof of the pudding and all that: within a couple of hours of signing the memo, the pink copy is back on my desk with a handwritten addition from Cicero.

Paul, this looks interesting. Come and have a chat. C.

An hour after that I'm writing a brand-new case number in the big green book: Samji Industries Limited, Growth Capital, £125,000. But this time I get to write my name in the rollcall of Birmingham controllers. I fill in and send off the form to request an industrial adviser visit.

Is Samji Industries a good business? I really have no idea. That's not to say I'm just shunting the decision off to Industry Department or to Cicero as the one who will have to sign the Submission – how dare you? It's just that I'm new and they represent a useful safety net against my inexperience. Anyway, if the industrial adviser turned down Latham with its super neat business plan and long trading history, the chances of him supporting Samji Industries have to be pretty thin. I don't mind, though; I'm just practicing, really.

February

There's a comprehensive 3i internal training programme for trainees that comprises several week-long residential courses, all run by senior controllers, Local Directors or other specialised staff. The first one is held in February – which happens to be the coldest one for twenty-three years – and the car I've borrowed, a ponderous family estate car, slithers and slides alarmingly on roads wet with snow as I drive down to the conference centre, a secluded hotel we use near the village of Creaton in Northamptonshire. I'm going to be there all week along with the eleven other graduate trainees from my intake, who have been dispersed to offices all across the country. It's a bit like fresher's week at university and there's a fair amount of socialising. The group includes the extraordinarily loud Scotsman, no longer in possession of a shopping trolley, but who seems perpetually on the verge of violence, particularly when he loses at pool; a part-time vicar whose jug ears make him resemble the FA cup; a tall, donnish chap with a stutter and a guy who looks like he's just arrived by tractor. Perhaps he *has* arrived by tractor, although I'm pretty sure Massey Ferguson does not feature prominently on the company car scheme. There's also a female trainee – a rarity – who's been sent to work in our Cambridge office.

Despite the constant hangovers, I learn an awful lot about the vulnerabilities of being a minority investor in an unquoted company. One of our in-house lawyers talks to us about the many ways you can expect to get ripped off by a management team.

They can simply start trading through a different company, leaving you with a large shareholding in Fuck All.

They make stuff up to get you to invest.

They refuse to pay your dividends.

They pay themselves enormous salaries, thereby stripping

all the cash out of the business and leaving you with Fuck All. They load the business with mountains of debt – Fuck All again.

They turn out to be totally incompetent but, since you have less than 50% of the shares, you can't fire them.

If someone offers to buy your shareholding for an enormous amount of money, they prevent you from accepting the offer because they like their life the way it is, and anyway you said you were long-term investors.

The lesson is that, if you're investing in minority positions, you can put all sorts of legal protections in place but, at the end of the day, if management is determined to rip you off then there's really Fuck All you can do about it.

By the end of the week I'm beginning to think you'd have to be mad to make minority investments in unquoted companies. I see why we have to be hard-faced and ruthless at times.

The highlight of the week is a formal dinner on Thursday evening, which is graced by the presence of our CEO, an elderly man with hair that looks like a plaster wig chiselled off a Greek statue. He makes a speech in the sort of accent you only normally hear on public information films from the 1940s, assuring us that the business is doing tremendously well, that we remain highly competitive on pricing and that, although it is true that we have lost the odd controller to the competition in recent months, we have nevertheless never lost anyone we actually wanted to keep.

He's either lying or deluded. In the bar afterwards we take a vote. Deluded wins by a clear majority.

Airport pensioner man calls me to say he's sorry for the delay but his business plan is now ready. Rather than send it to me 'cold' he proposes to bring it in person so he can 'talk me through it'. Am I free anytime this week?

I suggest he just put the business plan in the post and I promise to read it and let him know what I think. I successfully resist putting the word 'promptly' in there somewhere. He agrees, but I get the impression he's rather upset that I won't meet him just yet.

Monday morning WIP meeting. Samji Industries appears as an opened case and I get a whoop from the team. I try to look nonchalant but end up doing a shy smile, like a politician who's just been asked if he intends to run for the party leadership.

March

The gents' toilet is on the first floor between Cicero's office and the boardroom. There's one cubicle and two urinals. It's mid-morning and I'm comfortably seated in the cubicle when I hear Cicero and Callum come in, chatting. I'm not sure they realise the cubicle is occupied. They are discussing a deal someone submitted to Investment Committee yesterday that got bounced. The minute of the meeting has just been published and comments, tartly, that 'Committee had no appetite for the business.' This is apparently the equivalent of being called out in front of your primary school class and told to explain the meaning of the puddle under your desk.

'Well, it's hardly a surprise, is it?' remarks Cicero. 'A foundry? In the current climate?'

There's a steady tinkling as the two of them continue to ease themselves whilst contemplating the self-evident folly of the hapless controller concerned.

'Absolutely', says Callum eventually. There's the sound of fabric rustling, zips zipping, an abrupt gush of water from the taps in the handbasin, the sound of a door opening and shutting and footsteps receding. I'm left in silence trying to fathom the meaning of what I've just heard.

What's wrong with foundries? And what's the current climate?

This morning, Windmill is looking very pleased with himself. Clump has passed him the business plan of Bees Transport, a haulage company based in Hinckley. The reason he is so pleased is that it's a management buyout. And a proper one too – with an adviser and competition and everything.

Every controller wants to do a management buyout.

Management buyouts involve *proper* companies. For example, Bees Transport is making profits of £500k on nearly £10m of sales. A company like that could easily be worth £4m. Half of that will be borrowed from the bank, which leaves us with a cash out opportunity of £2m. They also have a proper adviser – in this case a well-known local accountant – which means the business plan is a thorough and professional document. It also means we're in competition with at least two other venture capitalists for the mandate – the right to finance the deal. Competing for deals is sexy.

We're never in competition for growth capital deals. The idea of another venture capitalist scrapping with us for the right to invest in Samji Industries is preposterous.

Nobody knows why the deal has been given to Windmill. The other controllers consider him amiable, not terribly bright and bone idle. He's been a controller for at least five years without being poached by the competition, which is deeply suspicious. After much discussion, the consensus is that it's a really, really clever plan to get rid of him. If the deal flops, he'll get fired. If the deal does well, the competition will mistakenly think he's a really good dealer and offer him a job.

Callum completes a deal in a specialist travel company on a Friday morning, which proves very convenient for Friday afternoon drinks. Our hangovers have barely abated when we arrive in the office on Monday morning to discover the company has somehow contrived to go bust over the weekend.

It transpires that the company had spent its new funds on Friday morning to buy forward airline seats for the forthcoming holiday season. Unfortunately, over the weekend one of the major tour operators announced a massive discounting scheme that drove down the price of package holidays overnight, meaning the company now possessed a stockpile of airline seats for which they had paid far more than they could ever hope to recover. The directors had no choice except to call in the receiver.

Bunny is a genuinely lovely man and management teams adore him. I like spending time visiting companies with him because he's very good at articulating what is good or problematic about a business. I learn a lot from him, not just about investing but also how to handle meetings. He's got this gentle style that makes him very easy to trust, which seems to be important to management teams. Possibly though, he's not ruthless or cynical enough to do well in 3i.

He's spent a lot of time working on a particular deal when it gets 'tweaked'. All deals over a certain size have to be approved by our Investment Committee, a mysterious and remote body of 3i directors that sits twice a week in London to pass judgement on deals submitted to it by controllers. Hence the reason why we call an investment paper a Submission.

The relationship between controllers and Investment Committee is one fraught with tension and mutual distrust. In particular, Committee seems to hold the view that controllers are fundamentally weak negotiators, always trying to give our money away too cheaply. Accordingly, it is prone to 'tweaking' the terms of a deal. 'Tweaking' is a euphemism for making a controller renegotiate a deal to obtain improved terms, usually in the form of an increase in 3i's equity stake.

One thing that I'm coming to appreciate is that the further away you are from the epicentre of a negotiation, the tougher and more brilliant a negotiator you become. What looks to the infantryman in the trench like a hard-fought, well-balanced compromise, always looks just like flagrant appeasement when observed dispassionately from behind the lines through the binoculars of distance. Sitting down in London, hundreds of miles from the action, the members of Investment Committee are invariably withering in their denunciation of the terms negotiated by controllers.

Clashes between controllers and Investment Committee are therefore commonplace and legendary, and there is a whole array of black humour and locker-room vocabulary around them: Committee is said to enjoy 'stiffening our spines',[4] getting us

---

4 Toughening our negotiating position.

to 'put our cocks on the block'[5] or placing our 'balls on the table'.[6] Needless to say, controllers – even the female ones, who you might suspect of being undeterred by threats to physical accessories they don't possess in the first place – dislike having their spines stiffened, their cocks presented for guillotining and their balls put out for public display.

Being forced to renegotiate an agreed deal because you've been 'tweaked' is horrible. Inevitably, the management team is incensed and you feel your credibility has been fatally undermined.

So. Bunny has had a deal 'tweaked'; that is to say, it has been approved by Investment Committee 'subject to an improvement in the terms'. He's called the customer in for a 'good news & bad news' meeting: the good news is that you have the money, the bad news is that we want more of the equity than we previously promised. This is a relatively big deal – £750k of cash out, which will take us a good way towards that fast-approaching cash out target of £20m for the year. Clump's not leaving this down to Bunny and has invited himself along to make sure we secure the management's commitment to the new terms, notwithstanding the hurdle that Investment Committee has decided to erect in our path.

We meet the managing director and the finance director in one of our meeting rooms. Although Bunny has not been specific about the purpose of the meeting, they must have picked something up from him because there's definitely an air of tension. Bunny looks deeply uncomfortable and tries a

5 Taking personal responsibility for the success – or failure – of an investment.

6 Taking a risk, or going out on a limb (if that doesn't invite too unfortunate a mixed anatomical metaphor).

little too hard with the opening small talk. Clump, however, shows no sign of awkwardness or embarrassment and does his over-the-top gushingly enthusiastic thing: he works them like a politician on a factory visit, pumping their hands vigorously, saying how closely he's followed the progress of their company over the last few years and how exciting it is that the opportunity has finally presented itself for us to 'do something really special together.'

The meeting proper starts and it's as if Bunny can't quite bring himself to deliver the message, because he goes around the houses burying it beneath a mound of caveats and qualifications and complex conditional assertions. It's as though there's been a murder in his living room and he's straightening the carpet, putting the vase back on the coffee table and plying the guests with tea and biscuits, but the one thing he's determined not to mention is the bloodied corpse lying on the floor. I can't work out what he's trying to say, even though I already know.

Suddenly the penny drops and the recriminations begin. The MD doesn't hold back and accuses us angrily of leading them on. Bunny goes into embarrassed, apologetic mode but Clump is having none of it.

'Look, guys,' he shrugs. 'You're just not worth it.'

There's a stunned silence. This is the man who, just a few moments ago, was telling them he's been a lifelong fan and was heartily looking forward to doing something special together. Now he has everyone's attention, Clump goes on.

'We look at thousands of deals like this every year. We know what a business is worth, much more than you do. If we say you're worth 'X', then 'X' is what you're worth. There's no point in sugaring the pill. Don't get me wrong: we're quite prepared to back you, but we need to make money out of this. So don't overplay your hand here. You're not going to get a better deal anywhere else. In fact, I doubt you'd get *any* deal anywhere else. My advice to you is to take what's on offer while the offer still stands and just be grateful you've got the cash. Your call.'

It is a brutal, barefaced, brilliant piece of bullying. The silence that resumes has quite a different quality to it. The two managers look at each other, shuffle their papers, make a show of thinking it over, but they are beaten and everyone in the room knows it. Bunny has gone a deep shade of red but just sits quietly, avoiding eye contact.

It's the FD who eventually speaks, saying they are obviously not happy and need to review their options. But we all know they don't have any.

I'm not sure what to think. It feels uncomfortable but you can't deny the effectiveness. Bunny's embarrassment was legitimising their protests and there was a very real risk they'd walk away in a fug of self-righteous indignation. Clump's intervention completely changed the dynamic. They'll leave the meeting with their noses in the air but after a face-saving delay, they'll be back to sign up.

Is this what being good at this job looks like? Clump would say, sure, he left some bruises, but in the end everyone got what they wanted: management got their money and we got our investment – nothing to see here. We're all grown-ups around here, aren't we? Nobody is forcing anyone to do anything they don't want to do, or that isn't in their best interests.

After the meeting, Bunny is quiet, even though it looks as though he's going to get £750k of cash out to his credit. He doesn't approve of Clump's tactics. But that's his problem: he'd rather lose the deal than be impolite.

Could I do that? I'm not sure I could. I might have to, though, if I want to get on. I don't want to be erased in meetings like poor Bunny.

The industrial adviser's report on Samji Industries arrives. I don't even bother reading the text and just turn to the second page looking for the recommendation.

Bloody hell! He's supported it.

To be honest, in my heart of hearts I had never believed this was a deal we would actually do. I read the report again just to make sure.

Definitely *'Supported'*.

I do a quick scan of the text.

This is a small company but one worthy of our support.

There's only one possible explanation: clearly my commercial instincts are outstanding.

I've still got to write a Submission and get Cicero to approve it but, with a *'Supported'* Industrial Adviser Report, that has to be a formality.

Oh my God – am I going to do a deal?

April

There's something in the economic air in 1986, a sense of gathering purpose and momentum. Old barriers are being swept away and new opportunities are opening up. The Bank of England abandons its traditional role of trying to micromanage the residential property market, and Big Bang not so much removes the traditional demarcation lines within the stock market as obliterates them. The UK government's privatisation programme is in full swing and culminates in the £9bn British

Gas share offering – the biggest and largest ever – accompanied by the innovative 'Tell Sid' marketing campaign that turns one and a half million people into first-time shareholders. Rupert Murdoch breaks the unions by shifting production of *The Sun* to Wapping. Hansen Trust, which has a reputation as a financially engineered asset-stripper, succeeds in a £2.5bn bid for Imperial Tobacco, a traditional industrial stalwart. The UK and France sign up to the construction of the Channel Tunnel and Gary Lineker becomes the most expensive British footballer ever in a £2.5m move to Barcelona.

We're just a small boat in a vast sea, but we feel the tide lifting us. Our financial year ends on 31 March and we sneak over the £20m target. What's more, when the official league table of 3i offices is published, Birmingham is second only to London on cash out. This is an impressive result. Moreover, it's a big jump on the previous year. 3i as a whole is growing fast and the only frustration is that the market is growing even faster. New private equity firms are starting up all the time, while existing ones are adding staff and competing strongly for deals. There's a sense of energy and optimism about, both in the UK as a whole and in Birmingham.

Cicero calls us into his office and we open a bottle of bubbly. Everyone is very pleased with themselves, particularly Cicero. Clump goes around the room telling everyone how he deserves all the credit. He's saying it in a jokey way but you can tell he actually believes it. I want to share everyone's sense of satisfaction, but I just don't feel it; I have contributed nothing, really. I know I'm only the trainee and little is expected of me, but that's not the problem. I want to feel what *they* are all feeling.

The trouble with starting your career by sifting all the crap is that you can end up thinking *everything* is crap. But I'm beginning to see that there are some nice businesses out there to invest in. For this I'm grateful to the other controllers who, for nothing other than a bit of company, are happy to take me along to their meetings. Salty takes me to a business way down on the south coast (way off our patch, which risks the wrath of the Local Director of the Southampton office, should he ever find out) that supplies plastic roofing to the major DIY retail chains such as B&Q and Sainsbury's Homebase. The directors are self-deprecatingly realistic about the quality of their product but refreshingly literate about business matters. With Callum I visit a family business out on the Herefordshire border, where they grow plants in extensive nurseries to wholesale to garden centres. These meetings are actually fun: it's interesting to see how quickly you can get to understand the essentials of what makes a business profitable and what its growth prospects are. It's also enjoyable to meet these management teams: they don't monologue or rant, and if you ask a good question they'll generally give you a good answer. In both cases, the companies need money and the conversations are quickly converted into growth capital investments.

Intuitively, there's a pyramid of quality when it comes to businesses. At the bottom of the pyramid there is an abundance of small proprietorial businesses into which you would never really want to invest. As a general rule, they exist simply to generate a living wage for their proprietor and are often fragile and poorly run. At the apex of the pyramid there are a few extremely high-quality companies into which any investor would love to invest. A lot of these are already listed on the stock exchange and have no need of us. 3i's territory is the middle section where there are some great businesses but also a constant risk of misjudgement and investing in something that is really in the proprietorial tier. The challenge is exacerbated by the pressure to do ever more deals: our appetite for cash out is limitless. And the more we eat the bigger our appetite becomes. The trouble with a voracious and undiscriminating appetite, though, is that you can easily find yourself eating something that makes you sick.

Cicero sets our cash out target for the year to March 1987 at £25m. It's ambitious.

The ache to complete a deal is becoming acute. I'm pinning all my hopes on Samji to break my duck.

Airport Man's business plan arrives in the post. Frankly, it's hard to see what took him so long and what he has been so meticulously researching. It's more a folder than a business plan; there are photocopies of various newspaper articles about growth in air travel and a copy of an extract from some book about managing successful ventures, some slogans from which have been marked up in yellow highlighter.

> 'THINK GLOBAL ACT LOCAL.'
> 'Management is doing things right; leadership is doing the right things.'
> 'Think outside the box.'

There's also a very precise handwritten diagram of a wooden pallet, annotated neatly in pencil, with measurements and with the cost of each component labelled clearly. Attached to the front of this assortment is a letter, addressed to me, anticipating that I am likely to have lots of questions and saying he is looking forward to meeting me in person. The letter also states that the funding required for the project will be precisely £4,567.89 (including a provision for contingency). The fact that the numbers are a precisely ascending sequence of digits does not escape my attention and I wonder, not for the first time, if I am being set up by some of my colleagues. I wouldn't put it past them and glance around suspiciously, but nobody seems to be paying me any particular attention.

I make the call and explain that it is not something we can help with, not least because the amount is significantly below our minimum investment threshold. In the stony silence that follows I recognise my faint feeling of discomfort as guilt. Which is quite absurd, of course, but the feeling persists.

There are muffled murmurings at the other end, as if the caller has placed his hand over the receiver, and I surmise that he's discussing the situation with the wife who started this whole thing off by buying him the bloody binoculars. Then the hand is removed and he comes back on the line clearly.

'I wish to make a complaint.'

These people really *are* like bloody cockroaches.

I'm writing the Submission for Samji but get stuck on how much of the equity to ask for. There has to be some technique or method for arriving at the right number, but I have no idea what it is. I could ask, I suppose.

On second thought, I decide to just put a number down and then debate it with Cicero when I discuss the Submission with him.

I put down 25% but, as I look at it on the page, I realise it looks suspiciously like I've just landed on the number halfway between 0% and 50%. After a moment's reflection, I change it to 30% to make me look like a tough negotiator.

I spend days crafting the Submission and adjusting the numbers; I can tell Alex is getting annoyed by the number of amendments I keep making. Eventually, though, I take a deep breath and settle on a final version. Alex prints it out on posh paper, which I have to sign, and sends it off to Cicero. I expect I'll get a summons to discuss it.

Within an hour it's back on my desk, signed and stamped: Approved.

Cicero
Local Director
Birmingham

He didn't want to discuss the deal or even enquire how I got to the equity percentage.

I am obviously deeply gifted at this.

Clump takes me to a GE meeting at an old family company. It takes place in an oak-panelled boardroom. The management team comprises a silver-haired distinguished chairman, a broad-shouldered MD with a face as bright as a tomato and a sharp-featured finance director.

It's an early start, and only half an hour into the meeting I begin to experience a worrying gurgle in my bowels and the urgent need for a toilet visit. I try to suppress it, but the gurgling won't calm itself. The bad news is that the chairman clearly likes the sound of his own voice, so I start to panic that I'm in for a long and increasingly uncomfortable wait. Luckily there's a slight pause in the monologue. Almost with a yelp of relief,

I seize the moment to intervene and enquire where I might find the gents. Expecting to be directed out into the corridor, the FD gestures towards a door within the room instead. I hadn't actually noticed it before, because it's fully integrated into the oak panelling pretty much right next to me. Leaving the boardroom table, I open the door curiously and peer inside to see, neatly tucked away, a single toilet and tiny handbasin in avocado and cream, smelling fresh and clean.

Awkward.

The partition might look like oak but it must be fake because I can still hear the conversation going on between Clump and the management team as clearly as if I was still in the room. The problem is that, if I can hear them, they can hear me. I do what I can to suppress the noise, including putting a layer of paper down on the surface of the water, but the easement isn't exactly a quiet affair and, after the first wave of cramping passes, I'm left steaming in a quiet, hot smog of embarrassment. I feel a pressure to keep things brief in the hope they'll just assume I'm having a tinkle, as if that somehow mitigates the humiliation – although I strongly suspect that ship has already sailed. There's a window barely big enough to get my fist through, but I open it anyway to try and relieve some of the smell. It doesn't seem to make much difference. If the opening was big enough, I'd be sorely tempted to climb through it and run away. I focus on trying to get on with things, but the risk is that I don't see things through and find myself obliged to interrupt the meeting again at a later point and announce the need for a refresher. Which would be even more excruciatingly embarrassing.

Actually, *'refresher'* is a poor choice of words. I've generated a real stinker and when it's finally finished I'm cocooned in a bubble of intense and deeply unpleasant fumes. I hope the furnace of shame emanating from my face isn't sufficient to set the air alight, in which case the only things that would emerge through the oak-panelled door would be a highly toxic ball of flame and a charred skeleton. I notice an aerosol air freshener and give it several long squirts, the sharp, sibilant sound of which must be easily overheard next door. I might as well be broadcasting SOS in Morse code squirts. When I finally unlatch the door and step back into the boardroom, a gust of the offensive, pungent aroma – now delicately laced with hints of lily of the valley – gushes past me and balloons into the room. The conversation stops and I sheepishly resume my seat at the table. The management team are polite enough to pretend not to have heard or noticed anything, but Clump has a huge smirk on his face and makes an ostensible show of sniffing the air.

'Curry last night, was it, Paul?'

May

There is a particular day in May 1986 when management buyouts become highly fashionable.

3i has been plugging away at management buyouts since the mid-1970s, mainly involving small unwanted subsidiaries of industrial groups where the only buyers are the managers who run them. They are fun deals to do and usually deliver a good chunk of cash out. The evidence also seems to be that they are very profitable, not least because the management teams invariably manage to buy the businesses at a knock-down price. There are one or two local advisers, accountants or solicitors who have cottoned on to this trend early and start regularly bringing us management teams who want to mount a buyout. The typical value of a deal is somewhere between £2m-£5m – a large deal for a regional office. Anything over £10m is officially classified as a 'large MBO' and we are supposed to pass these on to London Office, because allowing a regional controller to handle a large MBO is thought to be as sensible as throwing the keys for a combine harvester to a fifth-century agricultural peasant.

In May 1986 it hits the headlines that a management team has bought out Premier Foods from Cadbury Schweppes for £97m. It isn't just the size of the deal that is attention-grabbing; it's the fact that it's a local business. Cadbury Schweppes is based and headquartered in Birmingham, and so is Premier Foods. Nobody seriously believes we would have been a credible choice of investor in a transaction like that, but the fact that it's on our doorstep stings anyhow. The deal was done with funding from Bankers Trust, no doubt because American banks are way ahead of the British when it comes to large leveraged transactions.

By lunchtime our telephones are jangling with calls from the managing directors of local business subsidiaries who want to know how they, too, can 'do a Premier Brands'. To these callers, and to us in our little regional office, a £97m deal is about as attainable as a weekend trip to Mars.[7] But the *possibility* is infectious. Suddenly everyone wants to do a buyout.

Over the next couple of years, the MBO bandwagon really starts to roll. Venture capital firms just aren't supposed to make gigantic bids for publicly-listed corporations, but in the US in 1988 the CEO of RJR Nabisco mounts a $25bn management buyout and walks away with a $60m golden parachute when the

---

7 Today this would only be classified as a 'mid-market' deal, and not a particularly large one at that. Sometime in the 1990s the British Venture Capital Association changed the definition of 'large MBO' from >£10m to >£100m!

MBO bid is topped by KKR, a venture capital firm. It's a deal that shocks the world of corporate finance and soon you can read the full inside story in the best-selling book *Barbarians at the Gate*. In 1989, the mega-deal comes to the UK in the form of the £2.2bn buyout of Gateway Supermarkets (the new company is branded Isosceles). In 1990, the managing director of Premier Foods, Paul Judge, who had personally invested only £90,000 in his own management buyout, sells out for a personal fortune of £100m. In the UK in 1984, BVCA[8] members invested just £29m in 87 MBOs but, by 1990, those figures go up to £867m in 333 deals.

MBO fever has arrived.

Now I have to put the deal to the Samjis.

There's a standard 3i offer letter that sets out the terms and lists dozens and dozens of restrictions and provisions to prevent us ending up with Fuck All. I laboriously and methodically work through it, filling in all the required details, and get it approved by our Legal Department. I could just send it in the post, but this is considered poor form; the recommended approach is to visit the management and talk them through it. I feel the slow, sinister shadow of the Equity Panic Button creeping up behind me. That casual decision to incorporate a 30% equity stake in the proposal suddenly seems rather brave, but I'm rather stuck with it now. I could of course ask one of the experienced controllers to join me in the meeting, but that would mean losing credit for the deal. In any case, I'm getting used to the feeling

8 British Venture Capital Association.

of being totally out of my depth and, to be fair, it seems to be working remarkably well as a strategy so far.

It's a short walk around to the Samji workshop and I meet with Deepak and Samji Senior in the latter's office. I hand them copies of the letter and start to talk them through it, blurting out the equity part and rushing quickly onwards, like a kid sticking his fingers in his ears and shouting la-la-la-la to drown out the protests.

Except there *are* no protests. Neither of them bats an eyelid or even seeks to clarify anything. They listen to my interminable recital of the terms and conditions with respectful indifference and then Deepak thumbs through the offer letter until he's found the signature page and pushes it in front of his father, who signs it without comment.

Two weeks later the investment completes. I am disappointed that there isn't more of a ceremony, and in fact I don't even get to hand over a cheque because the funds are transmitted directly from our bank account to that of the company. But I do get another whoop at the WIP meeting when Samji Industries disappears from the 'Approved' category and turns up – solidly, immovably – in 'Completed'.

It's a bit like planting a flag on the moon with my name on it. GEs are transient things that buzz around animatedly for a while before disappearing out of the window on a zigzag flight path to oblivion. A completed deal is a stake in the ground, an inscription on a scroll, a painting on the wall of a cave. Even when I'm gone there will be a record, albeit a tiny one, in 3i's official history that we – that I – made an investment in Samji Industries Limited. Curiously I feel absolutely no fear whatsoever. It doesn't occur to me for a moment that anything could or will go wrong.

Apparently it's common in the industry to announce the completion of a deal by taking out a small advert in the press. The advert just lists the name of the company, the amount raised, the venture capital firm and the names of the advisers. They're called 'tombstones' because that's what they look like.

Disappointingly for me, the deal is too small to merit a public announcement. There'll be no tombstone for Samji Industries.

I know we have a formal complaints procedure but I have no idea what it is, so I make one up. I suggest to Mr Polite Pallet Man that he write in with the nature of his complaint, and I will forward it to the appropriate authority.

Yes, I really say that: appropriate authority. It just popped out.

A couple of weeks after the investment in Samji Industries completes, I am deeply honoured to be invited to Deepak's wedding.

The wedding takes place in a disused factory, transformed by means of a liberal deployment of exotic soft furnishings into an impressive imitation of an Indian temple. Only the rattling of the clapped-out Victorian-era central heating pipes, and the gusts of cold rain being catapulted against the loose iron-lattice windows, serve notice that we are not in the sultry foothills of the Punjab, but rather the industrial suburbs of Birmingham. A sour, cold smell of neglect is transiently suppressed by the warmer scents of jasmine and frangipani. Everyone is speaking Hindi and seems to be related, so I feel a bit excluded, but Samji Senior generously devotes himself to my welfare for the evening. He introduces me to lots of people with ungraspable names and there's plenty of smiling and nodding. He does his best to entertain me but his English is so broken that his efforts at conversation teeter haphazardly along a line between incomprehensible and incoherent. Of the groom himself, or the bride, I see little except from a distance.

I do feel something of a spare part, but that's more than compensated for by the warmth of the inclusive gesture of inviting me. I'm subsumed by a fuzzy happy feeling of having formed a strong bond with this authentic family business. Although, to be fair, I've also had a fair bit to drink ...

All in all, though, it is a very lovely and indeed spectacular wedding. Must have cost them a pretty penny.

5

HARD YARDS

'Success is stumbling from failure to failure with
no loss of enthusiasm.'

Winston Churchill

Two weeks later

My telephone rings and the caller, who has a soporific and
slightly comic Brummie twang in his voice, explains that he's
calling from Lloyds Bank. He is responsible for the Samji Industries account and he's ringing to inform me that, as there are
insufficient funds in the company's bank account, a large cheque
has been refused and the account frozen. He confides in passing
that this is not the first time there has been a problem with Samji
Industries presenting cheques that have no prospect of clearing.

Such is my naivety that at first it doesn't sound too bad; I am
sophisticated enough to know that there are inevitably many
bumps on the roads travelled by small companies. I vaguely
feel that the point of the call is to admonish me obliquely, like
the father of a wayward child being chided for bad parenting.

The caller keeps referring to 'the Bank' in the third person and my imagination can't help but conjure up a joyless, censorious bank official: dark-suited, wing-collared and bespectacled with horn-rimmed half-glasses, scratching out – with a quill pen on velour parchment – a stern reprimand addressed jointly to myself and the directors of Samji Industries Limited. I almost snigger. Then he gives me the name and contact details of the receiver and I realise it's a lot more serious than that. The company has actually – really – just gone bust. It feels like someone is squirting several quarts of battery acid right into the pit of my stomach.

I admit that my first thought is not for the Samji family, or the company's employees, or the creditors who are about to lose money. No, my first thought is one of selfish, shameless, naked self-interest.

'Oh shit,' I think. 'I'm going to be fired.'

Curiously enough, the reaction of the other members of the team – the secretaries as well as the controllers – is amusement rather than shock or horror, mixed in with a sort of rough affection. As the news spreads, I feel like a young naval midshipman enduring the whoops and cheers of the older deckhands on returning from my first visit to a dodgy bordello, minus a few grubby dollars and my virginity. The £125,000 loss, everyone assures me, will be written off to the training budget.

Still, I have to break the news to Cicero. To my vast relief and eternal gratitude, he is practical and understanding, sympathetic even. Most importantly, he gives no immediate indication that he is about to dismiss me for gross misconduct. He asks first if there is anything that could be done to rescue the company – more money for example? His questions, none of which have occurred to me, make me feel even more inadequate: have I spoken to the Samjis myself yet? How big is the company's overdraft and how big is the cheque that has bounced? What are the most recent financial statements I have seen? Has a receiver already been appointed? Have I contacted our legal department for advice? In my shock and inexperience, I realise I have failed the most basic tests of investment management. I feel utterly miserable. The discussion is suspended for an hour to give me time to inform myself on these and many other points, and I disappear off to do so, feeling a bit more positive now I have some concrete actions to address.

It is less than half an hour before I'm back with the information that nobody at the company is answering the telephone, but I have spoken to the receiver, who is already at the company's premises shutting down the operation and making the staff redundant. It is abundantly clear that it's already too late for any rescue action and the only thing that remains is for us to process the formalities and for me to face the consequences.

The local accountant, who acts as the receiver, reports that it is difficult to know what happened, mainly because of the almost total absence of any accounting records. Our money just blew away in a blizzard of small payments and cash withdrawals. He can't exclude the possibility that the Samjis have stolen the money, but far more likely it was just incompetence: a huge backlog of suppliers clamouring for payment and a family-run business with no fundamental grasp of economics. Most likely the profits I had seen in the accounts were illusory, based on stock that was valueless or costings that were too imaginative to even qualify as guesswork. The accountant does note, though – as an aside and choosing his words with care – that the son who had been most active in the management of the business, Samji Junior, had been unavailable to contribute to the enquiry due to his absence on an extended honeymoon overseas. He understands that the son's wedding was a lavish affair and that may well have aroused our suspicions. But his investigation can neither confirm nor exclude the possibility that some or all of the funds had been used to contribute to the wedding costs. On the other hand, it does seem a remarkable coincidence that the wedding so closely followed our investment and that the bankruptcy so closely followed the wedding. No doubt we've wondered if we have a case for legal action, but he doesn't rate our chances. Whatever our suspicions, there's no hard evidence of fraud or misrepresentation.

It's with something of a heavy tread that I make my way up to Cicero's office to learn my fate. I had been somewhat calmed by the constructive tone of our previous conversation but am still hugely relieved when it becomes clear I am not to be summarily dismissed. Cicero makes a speech about 3i's aversion to 'witch hunts' when money is lost. Risk-taking is to be encouraged, not penalised, he says.

I'm excused if not exonerated. Mostly, though, I feel utterly foolish. The really crazy thing is that it had honestly, not for one moment, ever occurred to me that this, my first ever investment, could possibly result in failure and the total loss of the funds invested. The family had seemed so respectable and ... well ... sensible. I had taken them at face value. How on earth could I have been so naïve?

June 1986

It's appraisal time. I'm asked to write a self-appraisal, which I approach cautiously: I'm still not quite sure where the Samji debacle leaves me. Cicero did, of course, assure me that 3i doesn't do witch hunts, but just using that phrase can't help but conjure up images of public pillory in the stocks or being strapped to a chair and dunked in the village pond. To be fair, everyone's been really good about it. But I can't help feeling there's the residue of a bad smell lingering, like I've stepped in something. Losing money appears to be the equivalent of farting when your new girlfriend's parents invite you over for dinner. Obviously they're not going to *say* anything, but we all know they smelled it. And it's for certain that they'll talk about it as soon as you've left the room.

To be honest, I'm slightly grateful for the conspiracy of silence – I've never coped well with criticism or humiliation. On the other hand, I'm not sure I've learned anything. I just lost £125k of someone else's money and I feel really shitty about that, but I'm still not sure what I did wrong. It seems obvious with hindsight that the accounts were just a work of fiction, but how was I supposed to know that? I'm not shirking responsibility, but in my defence, I would like to draw attention to the fact that neither the industrial adviser nor Cicero expressed the slightest suspicion about the integrity of the company's accounting either. The accounts I used for the Submission were audited, which I had rather taken to mean they could be trusted. I'm aware that most of our competitors pay a firm of accountants to review the numbers, but we don't do that as a matter of policy. If I don't know how I managed to miss the fact that Samji Industries was in reality a steaming pile of financial manure misrepresented as an alluring Victoria sponge cake, how am I supposed to not miss it again next time?

Anyway, on balance I'm happy to go along with the 'not mentioning it' strategy, but the imminence of my appraisal throws the issue once more into relief. Should I go mea culpa and beat my breast in penitence? Or spin the failure as an upliftingly positive learning experience? In the end I settle for liltingly positive obfuscation:

On the whole, it's been a positive start to my time at 3i Birmingham ...

I don't actually mention Samji directly: *naturally there have been some disappointments and useful learning points.* It takes me four or five drafts before I'm confident I've achieved the right tone. It's the chess equivalent of opening with a bold knight deployment on the basis that, if things don't go well, I can always boldly move it back again.

The moment comes and I'm summoned to join Cicero in his office. He sits behind his desk studying my tortuously compiled self-appraisal as though he's reading it for the first time, which I know he's not. He looks up at me and his hands start to perform a complex minuet. He tells me I'm doing well, that all the early signs are good, although if there are issues they often don't appear until later on. He's clearly decided to match obfuscation with mystification and I, for one, am happy to go along with that. Then he tells me he has decided to transfer me to the Portfolio Team. It's an important part of my training to gain exposure to the portfolio.

He pushes his hands forward, palms flat and outwards as if warding off an unwelcome thought.

'You'll be thinking this is some kind of demotion as a result of Samji Industries, but I want to reassure you that is absolutely not the case.'

He's right. That is exactly what I am thinking.

'Portfolio management is every bit as vital to a controller's skillset as new business and every trainee should spend time learning how to manage a portfolio. You'll perhaps also be concerned that this means you won't have an opportunity to write new business but, again, that's not the case. A fifth of our cash out is derived from further investments into our existing portfolio, so you'll still have plenty of opportunity – and be expected – to find and do deals.'

So much for witch hunts: whatever Cicero *says*, it still *feels* like I've been dunked in the village pond, pronounced guilty as charged and exiled somewhere my misfiring incantations can't do any more damage. Being sent to the Portfolio Team may not be quite as terminal as being burnt at the stake but it will certainly keep me away from the flow of GEs. That's the whole point of course – I'm not stupid.

I try to put on a brave face and leave his office with what I hope is a nod of professional acceptance. Trying not to show my disappointment and humiliation to the rest of the team, I collect my things from New Business and trudge up to report to Speedcheck on the third floor.

Speedcheck starts me off by giving me 140 cases to manage. It's like being sobered up by having a huge torrent of mediocrity poured over your head. Half of them haven't seen a 3i controller in years, like decrepit parents stowed away in a nursing home: out of sight and out of mind.

July 1986–September 1987

To ease me into life on the Portfolio Team, Banter invites me along to a meeting with his favourite customer.

Stan Coles is something of a celebrity amongst the Birmingham controllers because he owns and runs a business that distributes soft pornographic magazines. It is a small business, less than three-quarters of a million in sales and barely profitable, but Stan has big plans. He is forever ringing Banter, his controller, with fresh ideas for acquiring an influential share-holding in WHSmith, which has a policy of not stocking what are euphemistically referred to as 'top shelf' magazines. His thinking is that, with a 25% shareholding, he could appoint himself to the board of WHSmith and force through a change in policy leading, so Stan imagines, to a lucrative supply contract. Stan is undeterred by the fact that a 25% shareholding would cost £75m and require, under stock exchange rules, his tiny business to trigger a full takeover. So, on a technicality, it isn't £75m Stan needs; it's more like £300m. Stan is a let's-cross-that-bridge-when-we-come-to-it sort of man though.

Banter, with a wonderfully developed taste for the absurd, is always delighted to take Stan's calls and hear of his latest wheeze for overcoming these minor but challenging obstacles.

One idea gets Stan in such a frenzy of excitement that for once he demands a meeting to discuss it. It transpires that Stan has spent the last few days reading *Barbarians at the Gate*, the story of KKR's leveraged bid for RJR Nabisco, and become infatuated – perhaps a better word would be intoxicated – with the idea of using junk bonds[9] to finance his bid for WHSmith. He explains that he is intending to issue £75m of junk bonds and wants 3i to underwrite the issue.

Banter, clearly wanting to extract maximum entertainment from the encounter, doesn't reject the idea out of hand. Thoughtfully, and with a remarkably straight face, he asks Stan what sort of interest rate he is proposing to offer on the bonds.

Stan has done his homework. 'Well, obviously we'll be receiving dividends on the WHSmith shares, so the idea is

9 A junk bond is a loan considered so risky the lender demands an exceptionally high rate of interest in return.

that we just use those to pay a rate of interest on the bonds. I've worked it out. That comes out to an interest rate of 3%.'

Banter pauses, as if weighing up the merits of the proposal. '3%? Okay, I see. I'm wondering, though, if that will be enough to attract investors. What do you think?'

It is Stan's turn to pause. He's not quite sure whether this is a genuine inquiry or just a subtle way to start a negotiation. Still, he's not an unreasonable man.

'I don't know Banter; you're the money man. What sort of rate of interest do you think investors would be looking for?'

'Well, Stan.' It's like Banter is confiding a valuable secret to a very close friend. 'There would of course be an element of risk, so I suppose an investor would be pricing for an IRR of the order of 25%-30%.'

The shock shows on Stan's face. That is ten times what he had in mind. He suddenly notices the term 'IRR'. Of course, he has no idea what an IRR is but maybe, just maybe, it's not quite the same as an interest rate of 30%.

'Erm, just remind me, what exactly is an IRR?'

Banter has an MBA and is very accurate on these things. 'Well, Stan, as you will recall, an Internal Rate of Return is the rate at which you discount future cashflows in order to arrive at a net present value of zero.'

Stan stares down at his little Casio calculator, which is lying out on the meeting room table. It doesn't have a button for 'IRR'.

Banter decides to put him out of his misery.

'Stan, I think you're going to need a bigger calculator.'

Stan nods. Humbled but not humiliated, he speculates that he can probably get one in Rackham's. Could it wait ten minutes while he pops out to buy one?

'No problem!' says Banter, breezily.

There must be a shortage of Casio calculators in the shops that day, as Stan never makes it back to resume the meeting.

I receive a surprise call from our receptionist downstairs: Mr Samji Senior has come into the office and wants to see me. I find him waiting attentively in one of our meeting rooms. His English seems to have improved remarkably. He apologises for the unfortunate turn of events and hopes I haven't got into any trouble as a result. As for the particular reason for his visit, he is thinking of writing a book about his experiences as a first-generation Asian immigrant entrepreneur – is there any possibility 3i might be prepared to subsidise him? £25,000 should be more than enough. He assures me, of course, that any financial contribution would guarantee we would be portrayed in a very positive light.

My initial impressions of Anne were that she was rather unfriendly, but she offers to take me to visit one of her portfolio companies and, still keen to learn, I accept. The company makes telephones out of Wedgwood china – yuck, frankly, although I can easily imagine one in the office of Clump's Fifty Mill Flipper, between the fish tank and the white shagpile carpet. The company is run by a married couple who are not exactly well-schooled in accountancy. When asked for the accounts, they hand over what is clearly just an excerpt from their latest bank statement. Anne gives them an extensive lecture on the difference between profit and cash but she's clearly confusing them with people who give a toss. When we look at the bank statement, though, there do seem to be an awful lot of negative figures where no negative figures should be. It seems the company has already run out of money but, somehow, doesn't quite realise it yet. It's like one of those cartoons where the character runs off the edge of a cliff but doesn't actually start falling until something prompts him to look down. Well, we just looked down.

When we get back to the office, we go straight to Cicero to discuss a further investment to rescue the company. It was Anne who made the original investment and it's understandable that she's keen to avoid a blot on her copybook. Cicero clearly doesn't want to sanction a rescue, but he isn't one to say no directly so the two of them just glare at each other over his desk while he does the pushing away thing with his hands. I feel like a child caught between divorcing parents who are working through a substantial backlog of unsaid stuff by not saying it again. The silence is as stifling and itchy as a nylon blanket in a heatwave. Cicero's not for moving, though, and the yucky Wedgwood telephone company is allowed to go bust.

Anne doesn't stay much longer at 3i, and soon leaves to take up a job as FD at another company. It's a shame, as there are very few female controllers in 3i. As I near the end of my time at 3i Birmingham, though, another female controller does join us. She makes an investment in a media company where the two male owners are in a gay relationship. There's a fair bit of quiet awkwardness amongst the male controllers about this – not to mention some deeply inappropriate, if slightly elliptical, banter when a pint is in our hands. The truth is that, well, this is Birmingham in 1989. Deep down – if we're being perfectly honest – a few of us are not yet entirely free of prejudice when it comes to investing in companies that don't manufacture things.

On my portfolio there is a company called Castings plc. It's a formidably profitable specialist foundry that is listed on the Unlisted Securities Market.[10] Our investment is in the form of an ECSC[11] loan, which are cheap loans available to companies who can demonstrate that they are sustaining and creating employment in heavy industry. Somebody at 3i had the bright idea of becoming an agent to distribute these subsidised loans as a means of getting a foothold in larger industrial companies from which we could identify opportunities to perhaps sell them an equity investment. It's rare I get to visit a proper company, and it's an enticing idea that I could redeem myself in Cicero's eyes by converting our thin relationship with Castings into a juicy equity investment, so I arrange an early visit to meet the managing director.

While I'm told that Brian Cooke is terrifying, I'm sure my outstanding diplomatic skills are up to the task. Forewarned is forearmed, so I stay resilient during the frosty welcome and factory tour. At one point we come across a rather ancient female employee in an industrial smock who is sitting next to the factory wall, from which is protruding a long, threaded bolt. Every now and then a forklift truck trundles up and deposits a packing case full of threaded nuts alongside her, which she proceeds to work through, spinning each one onto the threaded bolt. Her hands are spindly and knotted, blue veins tracing out a chestnut-tree shape along the backs. If the threaded nut spins freely, she tosses it into another packing case; if it gets stuck, it gets thrown into a rejects bin. Cooke allows me to watch for

10 Forerunner of AIM, the Alternative Investment Market of the London Stock Exchange.

11 European Coal and Steel Community.

a long minute and then explains. 'Maisie is our quality control department.' When I look at him he's got a completely straight face, so I can't tell whether he's joking or not. I give a half-chuckle but it dies in my throat when he catches my eye. As we walk on, I ask if she does that all day. He gives me a cold stare and says, 'she likes it.' Again, I can't tell if he's being serious or just taunting me.

We finish the tour in his office, and his secretary brings in a cup of lukewarm coffee and a small plate of chocolate biscuits. Righto, I think, now is the time to deploy my considerable charm and create some rapport. I am taking a bite of biscuit when he speaks.

'I presume you're here because you want to buy some shares in the company.' It is somewhere between a statement and a question. Still, this is encouraging. He's clearly a straight-talker and perhaps just wants to get straight to business. Licking the crumbs off my lips, I nod in the affirmative.

'Not interested,' he says. 'So you can finish your chocolate biscuit and then you can fuck off.'

Fortunately, not all our portfolio managers are as unwelcoming as Brian Cooke at Castings.

It is my second visit to the mournfully named Ayling Trucks Limited. Mike Ayling, the flawlessly courteous – and far from ailing – majority shareholder and managing director of Ayling Trucks, very much looks forward to regular visits from his nominated 3i controller, even though the particular individual charged with that responsibility seems, in Mike's view, to change rather too frequently to enable a sound and enjoyable relationship to develop. The company, which affords Mike a decent standard of living, owns a truck dealership franchise for the Stoke-on-Trent area. 3i invested some years ago and I'm the latest of many controllers to be asked to 'manage' the investment, which mainly involves turning up at moderate intervals to discuss the accounts, collect any outstanding dividends or interest and have a convivial chat with the owner about life in general.

At this time, 3i Birmingham has several hundred investments on its books, accumulated over decades. The portfolio is like a large fishing net that has been dragged around behind a trawler for thirty years. When you empty it out to see what's inside, the catch includes just about every species in the business ocean: car and truck dealerships, potteries, printing companies, engineering sub-contractors, aerospace companies, dyeing businesses, IT consultancies, horticultural growers, retailers, hotels and restaurants, galvanisers of steel, plastic extruders, even a few golf clubs and the occasional nightclub. There are commercial radio stations, uPVC window companies, distributors of nuts and bolts and electrical components, and general and specialist hauliers. In fact, it would be harder to think of a category of company that *isn't* represented. Another 3i office even has, mysteriously, an investment in two decommissioned Royal Navy hunter-killer submarines.

The portfolio is an education. It's layered historically, like geological strata. So you can look at each stratum and learn something about how we got to where we are today.

For example, the portfolio contains a lot of tax-driven investments from the 1960s and 1970s, resulting from the attempts of various Labour governments to find a way to make pips squeak.[12] 3i profited from this generation-long attritional duel between capitalism and socialism by inventing various ways for shareholders in private companies to sell shares rather than take dividends, as capital gains tax rates were so much lower than those for income tax. Many successful private companies were also landed with a huge inheritance tax liability (then known by the much gloomier title of 'death duties') when the founder died. Rather than sell the company to find the cash to pay the tax bill, 3i would offer the beneficiaries the opportunity to 'sell some shares to Edith'. I initially surmised that Edith was a genius marketing brand, conjuring up the image of a benevolent Aunty Edith soothing bereaved relatives with a cup of sweet tea and sympathetic words before delving into her handbag and flourishing a large cheque stapled to a rapacious share purchase agreement. However, it turns out that Edith wasn't an aunty, or even a person, but an acronym for Estate Duties Investment Trust, which is much less pleasing.

Through the portfolio you can also trace the evolution of 3i's efforts to find a formula for making money out of growth capital for SMEs. The original idea had been to invest in the wheat and avoid the chaff, but in the late 1970s and early 1980s 3i underwent something of a crisis of self-confidence and decided that trying to pick winners was about as reliable as trying to forecast the outcome of the 3:30 at Cheltenham. It was better to play a numbers game: just maximise the number of deals and get

---

12 Denis Healey was widely quoted as stating his intention to 'tax the rich until the pips squeak' when he became Chancellor of the Exchequer in 1974. In fact, what he said was 'squeeze the property speculators until the pips squeak.' Nevertheless, the misquote was a pretty accurate reflection of the Labour government's underlying philosophy, which went on to introduce income tax at 98% on 'unearned income'.

as much money out the door as possible. If most of the capital came back by way of loan repayments, even if a proportion of the investments went bust, the capital loss would be more than compensated for by the companies that, unpredictably, went on to become winners. This strategy was referred to by controllers as 'spray and pray', and was the equivalent of giving cheque books to a tribe of monkeys in the hope that one of them would accidentally invest in Microsoft in its earliest days. 'Spray and pray' was the primary inspiration behind those golf clubs, nightclubs, restaurants and, most likely, the two decommissioned hunter-killer submarines. By the time I arrive in 1985, 'spray and pray' has fallen out of fashion and we are back – officially at least – to identifying good companies. However, the policy of 'spray and pray' survives in the form of a legacy rump of businesses on the portfolio that we should never have got into in the first place, and that come to be known as 'proprietorial' – code for small, troublesome and difficult to get shot of. Within my first portfolio of 140 cases, probably two-thirds are proprietorial. These are the businesses I now find myself looking after.

Managing the portfolio is a numbers game. We have 400 investments to look after and not many controllers. The usual principle applies whereby the senior guys get all the interesting cases, leaving a huge tail to be swept up by the juniors. Many of these cases rarely, if ever, receive a visit or indeed even a telephone call from a 3i controller. If they do need attention, it's usually because they fall into arrears on interest or dividends, or are about to go bust, or need something from you, such as consent under our loan or share documentation to increase borrowings or enter into a lease or some such matter. But given the sheer number of cases on the portfolio, there's always something that needs tidying up. Being a junior portfolio controller is like being the maid arriving at the apartment block in the morning: there's always someone who had a party the night before and upset the ashtray on the sofa.

However, most companies we invest in just quietly get on with their largely undramatic lives, paying their interest and dividends but never really growing much in value. Ayling Trucks is typical. It's a stable enough business, comfortably paying off our loan without any evident sense of financial stress but at the same time without showing any inclination of growing to a point where our 20% shareholding might actually be worth something. It is a lifestyle business, the fundamental purpose of which is to provide a comfortable living for Mike himself. But what Mike lacks in drive and ambition, he makes up for in geniality. As soon as I arrive he directs one of his underlings to wash my car, which never fails to make me feel quite presidential. Over a cup of coffee, we quickly review the latest accounts – a task quickly dealt with. Mike is inquisitive and likes to think of himself as something of a student of business. There is always a well-read copy of that day's *Financial Times* on his desk and he likes to quiz me thoughtfully and intelligently about the prospects of listing his company on the London Stock Exchange. I always struggle to find a way to let him down gently.

Diplomacy has its payoffs, though. One day, Mike calls me and says he has the opportunity to buy the freehold of his property. He could get a loan from the bank but he'd much rather give the business to me. It's a simple deal and I get £130k of cash out. Kerr-ching!

Why won't you give me a divorce?

3i MEMORANDUM

From: **Banter**
To: **File**
Date: **25th July 1986**
Subject: **Machsize Limited**

I visited this portfolio company on 22nd July. Our investment now comprises a shareholding of 15% (original cost: £7k), our £100k loan having been fully repaid some three years ago out of the proceeds of the sale of part of the property. The primary purpose of my visit was to obtain up-to-date financial information and to collect outstanding participating dividend arrears of £14k.

On arrival at the company's premises, I was greeted by the managing director who asked me a question: what, he enquired, do penguins and 3i controllers have in common? I admitted that I didn't know. He replied that they can both stick their bills up their arses.

I made every effort to engage in a meaningful discussion about the relationship between the company and 3i but the MD said the only relationship he's interested in is the one where we give him our shares back and fuck off.

'It's a joke, right? He didn't really say that?'

Banter is skinny and skeletal and when he finds something funny – and Banter finds almost everything funny – he has a deep rich laugh that racks his body so hard he can hardly speak.

I am not sure whether that was a yes or a no.

Post-investment encounters with our proprietorial portfolio are often unfriendly and difficult. Taking on an investment is not a purchase that necessarily gives enduring pleasure, like buying a luxury car or an item of jewellery. There's a burst of gratitude and relief as the money arrives in the bank account, but that soon fades. Then it can become as if you had a party the night before and, in a flush of intoxicated bonhomie, invited one of the guests to move in with you. A week later their toothpaste is in the bathroom, their shoes in the hallway and you're somehow expected to buy them food and cook them regular dinners. The umbrage grows: you start by making barbed comments about their irritating habits, progress to hiding their stuff in the attic and end up doing really immature things to make their life so unbearable they'll offer to leave. In 3i's case, this manifests itself as a demand to buy back the shares that were sold to us. But we have a strict policy against this, fearful that management have a buyer in the wings offering a better price for the shares. Confronted with our refusal to depart on agreed terms, management resort to finding ways to make our lives as uncomfortable as possible. One favourite tactic is to refuse to pay dividends or even supply financial accounts. It may not be terribly effective at making us leave, but to an owner-manager brewing up a simmering fug of resentment, it can be bloody satisfying.

Managers also often come to believe they were duped into taking our money in the first place. This can be particularly awkward when, in fact, they were. Clump in particular has a reputation for suggesting to management, when chasing a slice of cash out, that dividend payments are merely 'optional' or even that we would only ever take up our shareholding if the company ran into trouble.[13]

To mark the New Year, 3i produces a corporate calendar, branded with our logo, for distribution to all its customers and contacts. Each month comes with a cartoon and, rather out of character for 3i, they are all really funny and the calendar becomes a huge hit. The cartoon for January is a sketch of a board meeting where the chairman is summarising the discussion: 'So we're all agreed ... honesty is the best policy. Let's label that Option A.' I wonder if the cartoonist was thinking of Clump.

Banter eventually concedes that the memo is a spoof – he was just bored and wanted to see if Cicero ever actually read the Pinks – apart from the MD saying that the only relationship he's interested in is the one where 3i hands back its shares and fucks off. That bit was true.

To The Appropriate Authority at 3i

Sir,
I wish to make a formal complaint.
Yours faithfully,
S M Martin Esq.

---

13 We don't do it so often these days, but in the past many equity stakes were taken in the form of an option to subscribe for equity rather than an actual payment for them at the time of the investment. An option means you don't actually put the money in at the time you advance the loan. Instead you take the right to subscribe at some point in the future. This is fantastically cheeky since it means you don't actually put any risk money in until about five minutes before you sell, at which point you quickly subscribe and instantly sell the shares on at a profit.

There is still some unfinished business from New Business. Airport Man has written in to make a formal complaint. The letter, which is handwritten, isn't exactly specific as to the grounds for complaint.

The secretary who opened the post has to walk the letter around the office to ask who and what he might be complaining about.

I feign genuine curiosity and frown like I'm trying hard to recall if anything rings a bell.

'Nope,' I say. 'Sorry. Don't think it's anything to do with me.'

Debt Collector
Within my vast portfolio of 140 cases, there's a hard core that is constantly in arrears on loan or dividend payments. Most of these involve individually trivial sums – of the order of a few thousand or even just a few hundred pounds – but across thirty to forty cases, it adds up to a material amount and I am expected to make an effort to collect it. This means arranging a visit to the company to try to persuade the manager to cough up. It's about as far from 'helping companies with a distinct blend of financial and industrial skills' as it is possible to get. We might call ourselves investors or venture capitalists, but when you turn up at someone's office demanding money, you're just another debt collector.

But it is my job now and I get stuck into it. Speedcheck takes me to one side and gives me a pep talk about being 'commercial but fair'. I don't really know what that means but I think he's giving me permission to be tough, as long as I don't actually threaten anyone with an iron bar or anything.

Tough. Okay. I can do that.

I put on my mafia enforcer face and spend a good part of my first six months in the Portfolio Team criss-crossing the West Midlands, visiting industrial estates, receiving a surly and frosty reception and being told, with a greater or lesser degree of diplomacy, to fuck off. Nobody seems terribly intimidated by my scary face, and the arrears schedule proves more resilient than an acne spot on a teenager's nose. The point about dividends is that, by law, they are payable solely at the discretion of the directors and there is nothing I can do to enforce payment. If they tell me to fuck off, off I must fuck. If the outstanding money is loan arrears then we have a bit more leverage but, because management know that, loan arrears are much rarer.

I try to be tough about these debt collection trips but it's not that easy. I find myself in a meeting at Deed Engineering, a rather boring little business making turned parts for the automotive industry, which had been set up in the 1960s by the two owner-directors after completing their apprenticeships at British Leyland. After a promising start, the market had moved against them, as Leyland got tougher with suppliers and the industry began to restructure. Despite rampant increases in the cost of living, things never seemed stable enough to allow them to increase their salaries. I discover they are still on the same £8,500 salary they were paying themselves in the 1960s except, in real terms, it is now worth only a tenth of what it had been back then.[14] Imperceptibly but relentlessly, they have both passed from financial comfort to relative poverty. Now they are just clinging on in the hope that the business will survive and

---

14 Between 1960 and 1979, the annual increase in the RPI averaged 7.2%, reaching a peak in 1975 when prices increased by 24% in a single year. Look at it the other way around: imagine earning £85,000 a year and having it slashed to just £8,500.

continue to support them until the value in the property grows sufficiently to fund a decent pension.

I can't help feeling rather humbled by this tale. They seem like really good people: hard-working, with positive values and a strong sense of responsibility towards their families and their employees. I feel like a real little shit for coming here to squeeze a dividend out of them, like I'm a teacher snatching cake from a disabled child because there's a rule against bringing sweets into school.

It's easy in this job to become arrogant and snobbish when you sit in daily judgement of managers and their businesses, particularly if they don't express themselves well or obey the unwritten social protocols of the professional middle classes. There's no law saying you have to be articulate, concise or conversationally interesting. Running a small business – especially an unexceptional one – can be tough, financially unrewarding and require enormous reserves of resilience. These guys have been dealt a pretty rough hand and have stuck with it. They deserve admiration for that. What they don't deserve is for me to plunder their overstretched and overdrawn bank account for a sum of money that is totally immaterial to 3i. Empathy is not a helpful attribute when you're trying to be tough. After listening to their story, I don't have the heart to ask for the dividend. Not that I'm going to own up back at the office. I will just say that I asked and they told me to fuck off. Nobody will ever know any different.

Then a weird thing happens.

They write me a cheque for the outstanding dividend.

It seems to be because I've listened to their story and *haven't* asked for the dividend. Maybe I should drop the scary face and try listening more. For a moment I hover over the temptation to be a real saint and refuse to accept the cheque. But the moment passes and the cheque goes gratefully into my briefcase anyway. I try and assuage some degree of the guilt by persuading myself they would have been offended if I refused. It doesn't quite work though, and I feel mean for days afterwards.

As I drive back to the office, I find myself reflecting on the future of Deed Engineering and its two owner-managers. I have my doubts as to whether the property will rise enough in value to fund the purchase of their retirement lifeboat but find myself fervently hoping that it does.

Shipwrecks

And I thought GEs were bloody cockroaches ...

The company is called Parsonage Transformers, but the name is a complete misnomer. For a start, there's no cute rural cottage occupied by a ruddy-faced, jolly vicar – just a cramped and dirty workshop unit on a bleak industrial estate somewhere in the hinterland of north-east Birmingham, and a dog-eared and desperate managing director. And the only thing this company is good at transforming is cash into losses. Even the owner and managing director's surname – Chandler – evokes the wrong perception. The company doesn't work with wax, wick and tallow, but rather coils thin wire around a laminated core to make electrical transformers for incorporation into the electrics of plant and equipment. It's a respectable enough product but little Parsonage Transformers, in its tiny premises off the M6 motorway, can't compete with high-quality products from Germany or a wave of cheap imports from Asia. Sales are in steady decline and it's hard to see what anyone can do about it. It doesn't help that at some point in the distant past the company propped itself up with a ridiculously expensive loan from 3i. The cash that has been used to repay our loan would almost certainly have been better used trying to develop some new products or markets. But a series of hard-nosed 3i controllers, armed with the threat of putting the company into receivership, have enforced the repayment of most of the loan so that our investment now stands at only £15k, plus a small purchase of shares for £2k, although these were condemned to worthlessness long ago. It's all too late now. In short, the company is screwed.

I'm in Derek Chandler's disordered office for at least the tenth time in the last twelve months. I want to be sympathetic, I really do, but I'm finding it hard. He's not an impressive man; his thinking is hard to follow and he looks shabby and defeated. He's constantly arranging meetings with me to explain that the company has run out of cash (again) and to plead for clemency. The first time I met him, he asked us to put more money in; when I refused, I assumed the company would just fail. However, he managed to persuade Barclays to increase the personal mortgage on his house and lent that on to the company himself to plug the gap. That money lasted only a couple of months when he found an invoice discounter who would release more cash against the company's sales ledger. That, in turn, lasted only a matter of weeks and this time things really did look fatal – except that he managed to persuade the West Midlands Enterprise Board, a local authority fund, to stump up some further cash in the hope of preserving local jobs. That cash injection was exhausted within six months. Now I'm back in his office again and he's telling me he can't afford to pay the quarterly interest and capital repayment on our loan, which is due at the end of the month. Outside his office, there's a workforce of thirty to forty people, many of whom have worked for the company for decades and who, I imagine, will have pretty poor employment prospects if made redundant.

I know it's deeply inappropriate and heartless but the words that keep running around my head are *'why won't your company just die, Mr Bond?'*

Before coming to this meeting, I've discussed the situation with Cicero. The problem is that we only have £15k invested and, because we have a mortgage on the industrial property, in a receivership we'd get all our money back with any outstanding interest. So we're actually, speaking strictly from a commercial perspective, in a strong position. Obviously we won't do anything precipitate as long as the company is meeting its obligations on our loan. But, if they go into default, the best outcome for us is to allow the thing to go bust so we can get our money out and I can spend my time on more fruitful things. Derek is outraged by this. £15k is nothing to 3i but the consequences of enforcing our debt are horrible for everyone else: the company goes bust, he loses his house, the employees are all made redundant, the suppliers will not get paid and the West Midlands Enterprise Board will lose its investment. You have to admit that he has a point.

Cicero is not prepared to authorise a write off.

'Sometimes we have to be cruel to be kind. Management are just putting off the inevitable. Besides, we can't have word getting around the market that we're prepared to take a write off rather than enforce our security.

'You know, Paul, it's an essential skill of the job to be able to deliver bad news in a positive way. I know people who could sack you and still have you walking out of the room with a smile on your face. If you talk Mr Chandler through the implications of the situation, I suspect you'll find that he sees it's the right thing to do and better in the long run for both him and his employees.'

Oh thanks very much, mate. So it's not just a question of putting an entire business into bankruptcy; if I'm any good, I'll have them all cartwheeling joyously down the hard shoulder of the M6 in gratitude.

On my way to the meeting I rehearse my script. I'm going to set out the commercial position carefully and logically and invite him to agree that the situation is hopeless and that, however difficult the consequences might feel, the best thing for all concerned will be to put the company into receivership.

I deliver my speech pretty much as rehearsed, but he doesn't smile, or agree, or get furious with me, or anything really. He just deflates visibly in front of me, like a third of the air in his body has upped and left him. His gaze shifts from me to the workshop, which is overlooked through the glass windows of his office. I make an attempt to discuss the practicalities of the situation, but he's in some place far, far away. Eventually I just slide back my chair, gather my papers and quietly leave. He doesn't say goodbye or even acknowledge my going, just keeps staring out the window.

A couple weeks later I am notified by our accounts department that Parsonage Transformers has defaulted on its quarterly payment, and I instruct our legal department to commence proceedings to serve notice and place the company into bankruptcy. A receiver is appointed and in due course recovers all our outstanding debt.

I feel bad about it, but that's too easy. The bottom line is that Cicero is right. Whatever we did or didn't do, the company was going to fail sooner or later. And why should we surrender our position just so someone else can benefit?

The time on the portfolio is hardening me up. I think that's a good thing.

Commercial but Fair

Like a marriage, the relationship between management and investor is often very lovey-dovey at the start. But when you've been living together for a while, tensions grow and sometimes you end up in a situation where your interests as an investor and theirs as a management team clearly diverge. So when there's a fork in the road – who gets to decide which way to go?

3i even has a corporate value to guide in this situation: we're supposed to be 'commercial but fair'.

Terence Libby is something of a regular at our business lunches. He is active in the CBI, a supporter of 3i, and a pleasant and energetic character. He is the MD and majority share-holder in Morris Engineering, which is on my new portfolio. The company is based in the familiar well-lived-in industrial unit on the outskirts of Coventry, although the reception area is unusually neat and tidy and there is an air of purpose and activity about the place, which immediately sets it apart from most of the companies I have been visiting. 3i had first invested about ten years previously and subsequently supported the company with a series of further loans. We hold about 25% of the equity. The company is a respectable size, financially stable and has always settled its loan and dividend commitments promptly and without complaint. Morris Engineering is a good customer.

Terence greets me cordially and seems happy to show me around the business, even though he must have gone through the same routine with dozens of controllers over the years.

The company carves out drill bits from steel and the workshop is absolutely crammed with dozens of different shaped machines clattering like a troop of mechanical monkeys. I watch, absorbed, as an operator clamps a blank rod into a machine, which is then offered up to a cutting edge tipped with an industrial diamond, which in turn proceeds to carve out elegant spiral grooves to create a finished drill bit. Terence stops a machine, pulls out one of the drill bits and begins to explain the complex helix geometry of the spiral grooves. What makes the operation particularly intriguing is that these are not CNC machines. The graceful arcs performed by the cutting tool are all directed, not by a computer, but by a complex mechanical arrangement contained in the machine. Watching the rods and flywheels flick, whizz and rotate is like gazing into a giant watch mechanism.

At the end of the Second World War, a certain Captain Morris of the Royal Engineers, serving in the occupation forces, stumbled across a German factory making drill bits. The engineer in him was deeply impressed by the unique design of the machinery; so impressed, in fact, that he decided to 'liberate' it at the point of his Webley revolver. Commandeering some army trucks, he got his men to strip the factory and transport the equipment back to Coventry where he had it placed into storage until he was demobbed. When he returned, he leased a factory unit and set up Morris Engineering. They do say there's often a fine line between entrepreneurialism and crime.

Some years later, Terence himself acquired the business with the assistance of 3i. Presumably Captain Morris had long since retired, satisfied that in his little way he had secured some small reparation for the devastation of the city of Coventry by German bombs in 1940.

Terence is clearly very proud of his business and is at pains to point out that a modern CNC machine, which could reproduce product anywhere near the quality of these purely mechanical machines, would cost so much as to render the business uneconomic. This does mean, however, that when the machinery wears out – which inevitably it will at some point

– the company will probably have to close. Although still some years away, he is already planning for that day and expects the sale of the factory unit itself will leave him with a decent nest egg for his retirement.

The problem is that this is a very poor prospect for 3i. We have no grounds to complain about the healthy interest and dividend payments we have received over the years but at the present time our 25% shareholding would be worth something. Maybe the company could be sold to a bigger group that has the financial resources to invest in modern machinery and would like to take over the customer base? But if the company is doomed to shrivel and eventually expire, then we'll end up getting nothing in a voluntary liquidation. Manfully, I try and have this discussion with him and he's perfectly civil about it but equally adamant that he has absolutely no intention of selling. He has carved out a good living for himself and his employees, and the last thing he wants is to be forced to sell the company with God knows what implications for himself and his workforce.

Since we only have a minority stake there's very little we can do to force the issue. We'll just have to sit by and watch as our shareholding declines gracefully in value to nothing.

There are a lot of cases like this on our portfolio, and they come with a looming awareness that, in the aggregate, we are surrendering a substantial chunk of value. Companies, particularly smaller ones, do seem to have a natural arc of value and the danger is that we buy in at the start, see it soar over the top and then watch in frustration as it slithers down the other side. There's a divide within 3i about this. The traditionalists believe this is an acceptable price we must pay for our 'commercial but fair' philosophy. This view holds that our 'long-term, hands-off' approach has such broad appeal that the additional deals we win make up for the fact that a minority of them will disappoint. But there's a small, but growing, vociferous clique who think we're just letting management take the piss and we have every right to be more aggressive about forcing a realisation. This clique is simply reflecting what's happening in the market: our competitors are shamelessly forthright about driving businesses towards an exit. They won't invest at all if they can't see their way to a cash realisation within 3-5 years and are perfectly happy to agitate as a shareholder to pressure management into a sale. To back this up, there's a huge swing towards taking majority positions – owning more than 50% of the shares – so they have the right to replace the management if they have a falling out over what are euphemistically called 'strategic differences'.

It's ironic really: most of our customers regard us as greedy bastards, whereas our competitors think we're gentleman amateurs who are soft as shit. I have to admit there's something quite wickedly seductive about the prospect of being more muscular. Too often as a portfolio controller you feel like the butler equipped with nothing more effective than a discreet cough or an elliptical comment. And we're all ferally competitive twenty-somethings with an overly elevated opinion of ourselves. We're just not temperamentally suited to be butlers.

Cash out

Portfolio management is not all shipwrecks and debt collections – I make my first investment into a portfolio case.

Leek Dyeing & Finishing is an employee buyout from a large corporate conglomerate that decided it no longer wanted to own a grotty old dyehouse right in the middle of the Staffordshire market town of Leek. So they sold it to the modest-sized workforce, at a modest-sized valuation. The workforce were enterprising enough to take out second mortgages on their houses to enable them, with 3i's support, to buy the business – also helped by a customer across the Irish Sea who guaranteed some contracts and put up some of the purchase consideration. The customer was called Crepe Weavers, which took a third of the shares and a seat on the 'board'. Their representative, Jim McBride, is constantly ringing me to complain, in a broad Belfast accent, about the shockingly lax approach to corporate governance. Except that when he announces himself on the telephone it sounds like 'Crap Weavers', which always causes a titter around the office.

I see what he means about corporate governance, though. Management don't do suits or board meetings or weighty reporting packs, but they do offer a lovely mug of tea and a plate piled high with Tunnock's teacakes. On balance, I decide I prefer the tea and Tunnock's to an impressive financial report. My primary contact is the finance director, Peter Moran, who always greets me in cardigan and slippers. There are seven or eight other directors, which in fact comprises the bulk of the entire workforce. Visiting the old dye house itself is like a tour of the set of a Hammer House of Horror movie, with vats of foaming, bubbling, green and yellow liquids giving off unspeakable stenches as they are stirred by one of the share-holder directors. It is a capital-intensive business; there is always some piece of kit or other to replace and, as the profits neither go up or down, they rely on a regular flow of loans from 3i – like roughage in a diet to keep the bowels moving – to keep their cash flow smooth. 3i is to them a credit card, the balance on which never gets paid off.

I arrange a further loan of £125k for them. The important thing is not to ask too many questions about the risks of perpetually using new debt to replace old. They are nice guys and, when all is said and done, cash out is cash out.

I hear, many years later, that the old dye house is eventually bought by a national supermarket chain, demolished and replaced by a low-rise supermarket where, no doubt, the former workers now do their weekly grocery shop with nothing more to threaten the sensibility of their nostrils than the aroma of the cheese counter. Apparently the worker-directors all do very well out of the deal, which makes me feel happy inside.

Exits

A successful realisation of an investment should be like Christmas: a time of joy and goodwill to all men.

Looking at the body language of Eddie Hargrave, I wouldn't say there was much joy and goodwill in evidence. More a sort of howling exasperation.

Eddie is a big, cuddly man with a warming smile. Come to think of it, it would be easy to see him dressed up as Santa, doling out presents to excited toddlers. His company, which is on my portfolio, distributes pharmaceutical products to chemists and independent retailers. The company makes a decent profit but there's no doubt Eddie works hard and, since the margins of the business are so wafer-thin, there's a constant shadow as to what a serious recession or loss of a major customer might do to the business. When a large national pharmaceutical distribution company stepped up and made a decent takeover offer, Eddie didn't think too long before accepting it. We're not talking Bill Gates level wealth here: the offer is for £1.25m. 3i has a 20% shareholding, but that still leaves Eddie with £1m – a life-changing sum for him. It's a good return for 3i, too, as our loans will be paid back by the new owner and we will get to exchange our shares, for which we paid less than £10k, for a cash sum of £250k.

Understandably, Eddie was in a very good mood when he called me to pass on the news. I winced, knowing I was going to have to dampen his spirits. Now we are sitting in the claustrophobic office on the ground floor at the back of Colmore Row and the normally placid Eddie is getting seriously pissed off with me.

It's 3i's policy never to accept the first offer that comes in. There's sound commercial logic for this: it's common sense to at least check around to see if another buyer might either offer more or at least stampede the first buyer into upping their offer. But Eddie, understandably enough, is struggling to see past the cheque for £1m now dangling in front of his nose like a juicy raw steak in front of a starving coyote. He's worried that putting the buyer into an auction process will piss them off, they'll walk away and he'll end up losing the deal. My assurances that this won't happen sound hollow, even to me. After all, I don't know. I've never handled an exit before and am just parroting the party line.

There's another problem: the buyer is expecting all the shareholders to sign up to warranties, which are legally-binding promises that the company has told the truth about its financial position. 3i, as a matter of policy, refuses to sign them. Again, there's a sound commercial logic to this. If the new owner ends up disappointed with its acquisition, it would be too tempting to launch a legal action against wealthy 3i claiming it had been misled in some way about what it had bought.

Eddie, who I have never hitherto heard swear, calls me the choicest word in the profanity handbook. For a few moments I fear he is going to resort to violence, grasp me by the lapels of my suit and pin me against the wall. If he does, I suspect I'll go right through the flimsy partition and end up joining the GE meeting, which I can hear going on next door.

I have no choice but to insist, though, and we introduce a local adviser who succeeds in getting the buyer to up the offer to £1.35m. Eventually, after more than a few tantrums on either side, it is also accepted that we're not going to provide warranties. The sale goes through.

It still doesn't feel like Christmas, though. Eddie is not grateful for the extra £80k he's received as a result of our negotiating stance: he's still focusing on the £1m he might have lost. Once the sale completes, he refuses to take my congratulatory call.

Commercially it's a win but I feel a right old Scrooge. Surprisingly, it seems that making money can feel remarkably similar to losing it.

We've just sold one of our investments for millions.

It wasn't a case I would ever have been allowed near – an EDITH investment that had long ago repaid the bulk of our investment such that our very valuable shareholding had effectively been acquired for next to nothing. When the family finally decided to accept a lucrative offer from a trade buyer, our share was £5m in cash.

This is how it all works. We invest in hundreds of Ayling Trucks and Deed Engineerings and most of them go nowhere, except that they generate enough income to pay our salaries and cover our business overheads. Then, every now and again, a company in which we have a minority stake sells for an absolute fortune, which is where we make our profits.

It's less a question of backing horses than buying lots of tickets in a great corporate lottery. Since we buy such a large proportion of the available tickets, we're bound to win an equally large proportion of the prizes.

Another financial year slides past and, ambitious though it may have been, we achieve our £25m cash out target. The growth is coming mainly from more and bigger Management Buyouts. I've been doing solid enough work on the portfolio and even managed to contribute to the office cash out with a few modest portfolio loans. But the fact that the new business side is taking off just makes me anxious: I feel like I'm waving everyone off to the party while I stay at home to look after the house.

The target for the new financial year is £30m.

6

THE FRUIT MACHINE

'To be an accountant in the age of the
spreadsheet is ... well ... almost sexy.'

Steven Levy

October 1987

The team is forever changing. Bunny has had enough of being
bullied by Clump and leaves to become managing director of
a company that produces seeds for nurseries. None of us saw
that one coming. Callum has been promoted and moved to the
London office as 'number two' to one of the Local Directors
down there. Salty has been moved to our head office to admin-
ister the ECSC loan book and Windmill has been moved from
New Business up to Portfolio so he can concentrate on rescuing
Bees Transport, which is not going well. We have several new
joiners, two of whom had a fight on their first day over the last
parking space under the office.

The biggest change, though, is that Clump has left. Nobody is
quite sure what happened. Cicero isn't saying much and nobody

has spoken to Clump himself. One day he was there and the next he wasn't. Perhaps he's been murdered by a customer whose equity option just got exercised and his body hidden in a portfolio case – it could be decades before anyone finds it. We half expect him to appear at one of our competitors and haunt us like a malevolent ghost, but he doesn't. Probably just as well: with his flexible commercial morality and sociopathic charm he could do a lot of damage. Perhaps he really has decided to withdraw from worldly affairs and has gone off to join a monastery.

Cicero soon announces the new office structure. He's decided to become personally more 'market-facing', so there won't be a direct replacement for Clump. His new structure is to organise the office along product lines which means that in place of New Business and Portfolio we now have Growth Capital, Management Buyouts, Portfolio and Large Companies. Each team is headed by an investment director or senior controller. Needless to say, nobody is happy: people hate change and never see the opportunities, just all the things now denied to them. There's a lot of bleating and posing of snide questions, like what happens if it's a large company that wants growth capital. We're like kids being taken on a family holiday we don't want to go on. Cicero tries to ride all the sniping with dignity but we can tell he's getting really annoyed. He says that one sign of maturity, and an essential quality in anyone wishing to progress to Local Director, is an ability to cope with ambiguity.

It's good news for me, though, as it means I'm effectively back doing new business. I'm put in the Large Deals Team, which is being led by Despacito – one of the new arrivals, and a lovely man, but about as dynamic as a snail on marijuana. When on the telephone, which he is constantly, he likes to shove his free hand down the front of his trousers and have a really good rummage. In fact he spends so much time on the rummage that I rarely get to speak with him and, when I do finally secure an opportunity to seek clarification with him on what exactly the Large Deals Team does, he talks in riddles.

Funnily enough, I'm starting to miss Clump. I never felt easy with him, but his energy did drive us on and he was the fount of so many great stories. But the reality is that Clump was of a different era and his departure could only ever have been a matter of time. The future is not chutzpah, demonic charm, misdirection and bromantic obsessions with dodgy 'entrepreneurs'. The future is professional and ethical.

And ever so slightly duller.

I'm desperate to get some deals under my belt but it's just not that easy. I've spent the last year running around the portfolio clearing up the mess left by other controllers and have had no opportunity to build relationships with any of the top advisers. It's back to taking GEs, cold calling and squawking like a hungry chicklet whenever a business plan comes in to Cicero. I feel like I'm having one of those nightmares where I'm trying to get somewhere but every time I catch a train or a bus it ends up taking me further away from my destination.

I resort to lending £1m to a firm of accountants. Okay, so it's not real venture capital or a management buyout, but it's £1m of cash out. £1m of cash out buys you a lot of respect around here.

I'm on a cash out mission now. I don't want to lose any more money but I have absolutely *got* to get some proper new business deals under my belt. But it's not as though good deals grow on trees. You have to be prepared to work with what you've got.

A business plan comes in and for some reason ends up on my desk. The company is called Central Motor Services and the proposal is to establish a Vauxhall dealership somewhere in the suburbs of Birmingham. Total funding required is £150k and the bank is willing to provide an overdraft of £20k, meaning the company needs to raise the balance of £130k.

From an investor's point of view, it's hard to see where the upside is in a car dealership. True, there is a stable and enduring market for the product and, like any franchise operation, you do get the benefit of a national brand with all the advertising and promotional support that entails. On the other hand, car dealerships are not very profitable and, once up and running, there are very limited opportunities for further growth. A good well-run car dealership might make a net profit before tax of 1-2% of sales. A single franchise might expect to make perhaps £15k-£20k a year after loan interest and tax. Once up and running, a business like this might be worth £100k. That might be respectable but it's hardly going to justify risking £130k, particularly if you're only going to take a 25% share of it.

But I'm on a cash out mission. I need deals under my belt. And there's now a business plan on my desk. There has to be a way to do this.

If I can't get the valuation up, maybe I can get the PELT down. If I can get the PELT down, then the amount of risk money in the deal falls and the upside improves accordingly.

PELT is a word unique to 3i. If an outsider hears it, they presumably think we're involved in trading fur and animal skins, but fortunately it's not that distasteful. What PELT actually stands for is Potential Equity Loss Total: the calculation of the money you stand to lose if a deal goes bust. Since we take a debenture, in theory at least our losses can be reduced in an insolvency by selling what's left of the assets. When it comes to calculating PELT, controllers can be very inventive: how about, for example, if the business is a seasonal one, selecting a balance sheet from the point in the year when working capital is at its peak? Another really good trick I discover is to press into service the government's loan guarantee scheme, for which we are an authorised agent. Under the LGS the government will pay us out 70% of our loan losses in the event the company goes bust.

So, I write a Submission proposing a £125k loan, backed by the Loan Guarantee Scheme, plus an investment of £5k for 25% of the equity. The use of LGS reduces our PELT from £130k to £40k. So we are now risking only £40k, but I still get the cash out of £130k and a 25% equity stake in the new venture.

Cicero still turns it down, though. Despite my skilful financial engineering, he's just not persuaded that a Vauxhall dealership is an attractive investment opportunity. He's right of course – it isn't. But there's a deal to be done and there's a cash out opportunity on the table – I'm not yet ready to give up.

I go back to the managing director and flagrantly manipulate him. He's not a dishonest man but he's really no match for a controller on a cash out mission. I tell him that we'd like to support him but the forecasts don't show sufficient potential to justify an investment. He gets the hint and says he thinks he's been guilty of being too conservative in his forecasting. I say that often happens. In fact, I explain, management often confuse forecasting for the bank with forecasting for an investor. A bank wants to see the worst-case scenario, whereas an investor wants to see ambition. He agrees that maybe he's fallen into exactly that trap and says he'll have a look again at his forecasts, to make sure they adequately reflect the true potential of the business.

The next day a new set of forecasts arrive on my desk, with materially higher numbers. I incorporate them into a revised Submission and send it to Cicero, who now signs it.

It's shameless but I doubt there's a controller who hasn't done it. In fact, I know there are plenty of controllers who've done it because I've spent the last twelve months on the portfolio managing exactly this kind of crap. That alone should make me feel guilty but it doesn't. In fact, rather the contrary, I rather feel I've earned the right to make some crap of my own. And I need the cash out.

I salve my conscience by telling myself that while, speaking strictly from a narrow commercial perspective, this is perhaps not a deal 3i should do, nevertheless I've been responsible for creating a new business and surely that's not a bad thing? I doubt it will go bust – at least not for a long time, when my involvement will hopefully be forgotten. Anyway, 3i can afford it. They should look at the bigger picture and consider it a sound long-term investment in my career.

The grateful entrepreneur invites me to a launch party at the new dealership. The invitation says it's a black-tie event so I mistakenly think this is going to be a stylish occasion and I invite a date. Big mistake. It's held in the dealership showroom and they don't even bother to remove the new and used cars with the white cards with the prices still on. The food is just nibbles comprising those cocktail sticks with pineapple and cheese chunks, and the wine – served in white, ribbed, plastic cups – is so tart it removes the enamel from your teeth. My date isn't impressed. After ten minutes she says she's popping to the loo and never returns.

PELT might be good for your cash out target but it does bugger all for your sex life.

Flagpole, our regional director, comes for a visit. Flagpole is the tall, willowy, patrician gentleman who had been so impressed with my advice on getting his nephew into Oxford that he'd endorsed me as a trainee investment controller. We all gather around the boardroom table, eat sandwiches and bleat. Despite being well paid and privileged to do a job that most people would die for, controllers are world class complainers. Favourite complaints include the intransigence of Investment Committee, the inadequacy of our salaries relative to the competition, the austerity of the company car policy and why we can't be titled something much more self-important like 'investment executives'.

Flagpole is used to jousting with lippy, vain controllers and nobody lays a glove on him.

'Controllers control the process. I think it's rather a good name.'

Like every organisation that lends or invests money, 3i has a system of checks and balances. Controllers find and do the deals; industrial advisers validate the business proposition and Investment Committee, or an individual with an approval authority, decides whether to make the investment or not. Industrial advisers are well-meaning individuals, older than us and with a business background. But, whatever the quality of their views on the business, controllers are always going to resent them for no other reason than because they are a hurdle that needs to be cleared and a standing insult to our competence. Having to involve them also complicates the process, as you need to explain their role to management and justify the delay – often several weeks – when everyone just wants to get on with the deal. None of our competitors have industrial advisers.

The approval authority is determined by the size of the proposed investment. Local directors have a modest approval authority (Cicero's is £150,000), which varies according to experience and seniority, but the bulk of our approvals are done by regional directors (deals up to £250,000). RDs each have their own unique personal style, and one of the tricks is to try and steer a Submission towards a more sympathetic one or away from an unhelpful one. Flagpole is relatively easy going and seems prepared to approve most things you put to him, although he's not averse to mild tinkering. He does, though, have a disconcerting way of whistling on the phone. Other RDs use the approval process as an opportunity to grandstand, showboat and screw over management teams. In other words, the role of approval authority attracts bullies like chum attracts sharks. Chief bully is Derek Sach, former Local Director in Birmingham and now something of a darling of the Tenth Floor,[15] who is known for intimidating controllers and demanding an improvement in terms as the price for signing off the deal.

If a deal is beyond the approval level of a regional director, it goes to Investment Committee, which sits twice a week in London – Monday afternoons and Wednesday mornings – and is basically the Tenth Floor including the CEO and finance director. At each session, Committee reviews up to a dozen Submissions, which means that each deal only gets their attention for a few minutes. We aren't allowed to attend Committee meetings and nor are our Local Directors because Committee members believe their commercial insight is at its purest when

---

15 Code for the cabal of individuals who run 3i, otherwise known as ExCo (Executive Committee). The Tenth Floor of the group Head Office in Waterloo is where they reside.

unchallenged by the grating persistence of an argumentative controller in hot pursuit of a chunky slice of cash out. So the workings of Investment Committee remain largely a mystery to us. There aren't even any minutes of the debate other than to record the decision: approved or rejected. The only occasions when Committee is moved to a more expansive commentary is when the proposition is considered to be so unattractive as to merit dismissal with disgust, such as the infamous 'Committee had no appetite for the business'.[16] Conversely, IC never ever publishes a minute that expresses delight at or enthusiasm for an investment proposition or compliments the controller on a good job in finding and winning the deal. The closest you ever get to a 'well done' is a terse 'Approved as submitted'.

Controllers are the huskies of the business, yelping and unruly but energetic. When harnessed, we are capable of pulling the business forward at remarkable speed. This suits the Tenth Floor because they are obsessed with growth, desiring to put more cash out to work and to build the portfolio. All the same, they don't trust us. Their dilemma is how to motivate us to deliver ever-increasing quantities of cash out whilst keeping us from pulling the sled in the wrong direction. They worry a lot about being pulled in the wrong direction. Their greatest fear is being buried in an avalanche of rotten deals. They're scared they have created a culture in which controllers would lend money to a corpse if we thought we could get away with it. They want us ferocious in our pursuit of ever bigger cash out targets, whilst fearing the loss of objectivity that seems to entail. They fear us 'going native', a phrase coined in the days of empire to reflect

16 Like Donald Trump, Investment Committee likes to refer to itself in the third person.

the concern that well-educated young white men from the home counties might freak out in the hot sun and go soft on the impoverished locals when extracting taxes. In investment terms, going native therefore means developing too much empathy for the management teams we are working with and, as a result, being insufficiently robust in negotiations. It is encapsulated in another of Investment Committee's favourite rejections: 'Committee considered the deal too good for management'. What they really mean is that 'Committee considered the deal too good for the natives'.

So, we suspect, the real reason why we are called controllers isn't because it happens to be a particularly accurate way to describe our role; it's because they don't want us to get ideas above our station. Controllers aren't investors – that would imply that we actually get to make investment decisions, which doesn't reflect where the real commercial judgement resides in the organisation. We're just processors. Like claims handlers in an insurance company.

Flagpole has a better idea. 'Perhaps we should just call you *salesmen*'.

We think he is joking. But a couple of weeks later a new controller joins from IBM, where he had been a 'salesman'. We call him 'Flagpole's experiment'. Flagpole will no doubt allow himself a quiet smile of satisfaction when, thirty years later, 'Flagpole's Experiment' becomes chairman of the British Venture Capital Association.

I'm given a new trainee to mentor. Rick arrives straight from university, although he looks more like he's arrived direct from Santa Monica beach in a VW camper van. He has bleached blond hair, wide and innocent blue eyes, and a general air of smoking something. As it happens, I'm being taken out to lunch by a couple of local advisers and take him along to balance the numbers. And – it's pathetic I know – to impress him. We go to the Midland Hotel where the waiters still wear bow ties and bring out the food on plates covered in steel domes. Rick promptly disappears behind a ridiculously oversized menu while I get through the business small talk. When the waiter comes to take our order two clear blue eyes and a mop of tousled hair pop up inquisitively from behind the menu.

'What? Can I have *anything*?'

The advisers, who are paying, confirm that of course he can have anything.

'Right,' he says ducking decisively back down. He orders the most expensive thing on the menu.

Every year, each controller is given a beautiful little red *Economist* diary containing an almanac of information such as sunset and sunrise times in Afghanistan, a league table of countries by GDP per capita and a comprehensive schedule of world public holidays. Into this diary we handwrite all our meetings and the names, addresses and telephone numbers of any useful contacts.

We have no computers on our desks and there's no database of anything to which we have access. There is no email and, if we want any information on an investment, we have to locate the physical file, pull it out and search it for whatever it is we're looking up. Microsoft Outlook is years away and Google even further into the future.

But information technology is gathering on the horizon and Birmingham office is chosen as the one to trial our new computer system, which for some obscure reason is called the 'CT system'. A team of technicians turns up at the office and starts ripping out floors and ceilings to lay cables, and dismantling and reassembling desks to accommodate huge heavy cathode ray computer screens, keyboards and desktop servers. Cicero tells us all to take the day off so those controllers with families stay at home, the rest of us go to the pub and Despacito – the Chemically Contented Snail – remains in his chair, telephone handset wedged to his ear, rummaging contentedly away as the entire infrastructure of the building is disassembled and reassembled around him.

We all hate the CT system. It's slow and clunky and all the pre-loaded information appears to be wrong. The girls hate the word processor application and want their Wangs back.

Plaster Wig, our CEO, pays us a special visit to hear our views on the new system in advance of the decision on whether to roll it out to the rest of the business. Cicero knows us too well, though, and realises this is the equivalent of inviting a flamboyantly gay man into a room with a posse of tattooed skinheads in Doc Martens. He's having none of it. He wants his office to be seen as progressive, can-do and enthusiastic, not a den of whining hyenas. He gets his secretary to type out a dozen or more positive statements about the system and allocate them to individual controllers with instructions to learn them by heart and be prepared to regurgitate them on demand. I don't get one, which is fine by me. Cicero is already more than a bit sensitive over this blatant exercise in spin so there's no upside to be had in provoking his ire further.

When the day comes, Plaster Wig is ushered into the boardroom, where we are all lined up around the table with our ties neatly tied and our suit jackets on. It's like the king is visiting

Downton Abbey expressly to interrogate the servants about the new-fangled gaslight system being trialled for Buckingham Palace. We all deliver our lines flawlessly and nobody says what they're really thinking. Plaster Wig departs, convinced the CT system is an inspirational purchase, while Cicero is happy because his team have come across in a way that reflects well on him.

The rollout goes ahead and is a disaster. All the other offices hate it as much as we do and within three years the whole thing gets scrapped. But by then Plaster Wig has retired and Cicero has been promoted. Welcome to the new age of information technology.

There's almost a mutiny when we're told 3i won't be issuing us with our lovely little red *Economist* diaries anymore. How on earth are we going to know whether the sun has set in Kabul, or that a neap tide is imminent on the east coast of Malaysia?

I don't know about you, but I've always found stationery delightful. There's something profoundly seductive about a fresh, crisp, as yet unscribbled upon, lined writing pad; a sheaf of neatly stacked white envelopes waiting patiently to be filled like white taxi cabs in a rank; or a loose box of virgin roller ball pens in blue, black or red. Put me in a stationery cupboard and I'm like a kid in a sweet shop. Put me in a stationery shop and I want to invest in it.

P K Stationery has two stationery shops in Staffordshire and big plans. The entrepreneur, Neil, wants to build a chain of 250 shops and has put together a business plan to raise the capital. To be honest, I warm much less to Neil than I do to his stationery – he is self-opinionated, bombastic and prone to monologuing, but these are characteristics I have already come to associate with the concept of an 'entrepreneur'.

Let's not be mealy-mouthed about this, though: this is a real deal. It has an entrepreneur, some existing trading data to support the business plan and it's a retail rollout, which is a hot space in the late 1980s. If there's possibly a way to do this deal, I'm going to do it.

When looking at a venture investment, there are essentially two things you need to know at the outset: how much capital does the project need and what profits will it make as a result? In a retail rollout, getting at these two numbers is far from straightforward.

The theory is simple enough: you start with a 'model shop', multiply it by the number of shops you want and then add the overheads you think necessary to manage the business. Neil reckons, from his experience with the two existing outlets, that each shop can be set up for about £50k and each shop will produce revenues of between £80-£100k. Extrapolating from these numbers, and assuming it would take two years to get to 250 shops, his business plan shows a business capable of producing sales of £25m, a profit of £3m and a funding requirement of £5m.

Well that's lovely but, sadly, also completely bonkers. For a start nobody is going to be daft enough to front up with £5m to an unproven entrepreneur, however stratospheric his levels of personal self-esteem and bombast, on the basis of extrapolating from two tiny experimental shops in Staffordshire. But there *is* a more modest and practical alternative strategy, which is to prove the concept by building up to a smaller number of shops, say fifteen to twenty, then aim to sell it to an established retail brand who would have the resources to realise its full potential. There are also some internal political considerations: I can't quite put my finger on why, but my instinct tells me that Investment Committee will have absolutely no appetite for this particular proposition. Realistically, I have to get the funding requirement down to £250k, where I might have a chance of getting Flagpole to approve it.

This all implies a serious reworking of the numbers in Neil's ambitious business plan. It's not just a question of calculating the outcome on the basis of fifteen to twenty shops rather than the 250 Neil wants to aim for. You can't open even fifteen shops on the same day, so you have to decide on a rollout period, which means costs, profits and cash staggering in and out like rugby players on a pub crawl. And trying to predict with accuracy which particular group of rugby players will stagger into which pub at what time of the evening and ... well, you get the point ...

The faster you schedule the rollout, the bigger the initial funding requirement becomes and the riskier the proposition, but both the funding requirement and the risk factor fall dramatically if you delay the rollout to allow new shops to be financed by profits from the earlier shops coming onstream. And we now have a budget of £250k determined solely by the arbitrary values of 3i's internal approval system. Manipulating all the variables to come up with a workable solution looks fiendishly difficult unless you have a degree in maths, and maths is not my strong point.

What makes this investment possible is a radical new innovation in financial circles called a 'spreadsheet'.

I saw my first spreadsheet on a clunky IBM personal computer just months before joining 3i. It had been demonstrated at a course I was on at Ashridge Management College, where I was allowed to play with it for just a few minutes. But we don't use spreadsheets at 3i yet for the simple reason that we don't have them. So it's a novel moment for me when I am in a meeting with Neil, discussing how we might massage the cashflows to make the investment case more realistic, and his accountant produces a floppy disk containing the spreadsheet on which he has modelled the cashflows and invites me to take it away and 'have a play'. That's like me visiting the cockpit of an Airbus 380, only to be ushered into the pilot's seat and invited to have a go at the approach and landing while the captain pops back to business class for a snooze.

On the way back to the office I find myself thinking about the new computer terminal sitting on my desk and wondering if there's some way it might be of use here. When I get back to the office, I crawl under the desk to where this large grey plastic box now resides; it has blinking lights and occasionally erupts into mysterious humming and clicking sounds, like there's a cricket inside conducting a choir of miniature Buddhist monks. There are various apertures on the front of the box, one of which seems to match the floppy disk I've been given. It's like offering an apple to a horse: you hold it out and suddenly the whole thing disappears down its throat. There's a satisfying clunk and a whir, and I resurface to look expectantly at the green screen, expecting something to happen. Which it doesn't.

Ok. So what do I do now?

I make my first ever call to a helpdesk and the person who answers speaks to me like an astrophysicist who's been put on bathroom duty, explaining how the taps work. He instructs me to back out into DOS, find the A drive and locate something called an '.exe file'. We go through the entire routine several times but end up with the same error message each time. It seems the bespoke spreadsheet package we have on our system isn't, in fact, compatible with Lotus 1-2-3. We are forced to give up, at which point he consoles me with the information that I wouldn't have been allowed to use it anyway because group policy is that no external files are to be loaded onto our computers without being first checked by IT department.

So I spend about a week teaching myself how to use the spreadsheet on our system, using P K Stationery as my guinea pig. I manually transcribe the key numbers from the written business plan into our bespoke spreadsheet and build my own model. It's almost an out of body experience: the outside world fades around me; everything else in my in-tray gets ignored; I stop answering the phone, forget to eat and go to bed at night wondering if there's a way to reformat a line of figures I've entered as a row into a column. The floppy disk from Neil's accountant's model lies undisturbed on my desk like an unopened box of chocolates.

Finally I get to the point where I have a functioning model, with a profit and loss account, balance sheets and cashflow all integrated, stretching out into the unimaginably distant future. I try changing some numbers and watch, awed and captivated, as the numbers cascade across the screen before settling down, like a fruit machine coming up with three golden crowns.

Even then, I realise this is game-changing stuff, the power to manipulate huge quantities of numbers in an instant without fear of arithmetical error.

With the financial model now written and functioning, I get back on task. How many shops can you open for £250k and what would that look like in terms of sales and profits? I just try guessing at first, and that works well enough, but then I discover a function called Goalseek. That looks promising. It takes a bit more modelling but soon I have developed a way to isolate the whole problem down to two cells: in one I enter the funding limit, and the other automatically generates the number of shops. I press recalculate and, like a regiment of soldiers falling in, the numbers all come into line. It looks like we could get to twenty-five shops over an eighteen-month period, at which point we would be running at sales of just over £2m and cash breakeven. That seems to work. It would be enough to demonstrate the potential to a buyer and give us breathing space to conduct negotiations.

We have a deal.

The next step is to pass the case over to an industrial adviser. Three weeks later the report is back. The Adviser is obviously also a stationery lover because he likes the concept, although he thinks the business plan underestimates the overheads somewhat. No problem! I just rework the model to increase overheads as a percentage of sales, the fruit machine cascades again, and this time three strawberries come up. We can probably only make it to twenty shops, but if we delay the rollout to 24 months we still end up at cash breakeven. That'll do. In my excitement I almost overlook the startling comment from the Adviser that 'if there is anything fundamentally wrong with this investment then I cannot see what it is.'

That should have been a warning. But I'm not listening to warnings. This is a real deal; I have a supportive industrial adviser's report and I'm like a rat that has spotted a signpost to a drainpipe. I'm not going to turn it down on the grounds of hyperbole, am I?

There's an eternal triangle thing going on between VCs, management teams and advisers. In an attempt to reinvent myself as sophisticated and well-read, I once tackled a Sartre play about three fundamentally incompatible people being stuck for eternity in a basement together. It's rather like that.

Raising venture capital is a big decision for a management team. It's a big, bewildering world out there and they don't know who to approach. They need someone on their side, when negotiating with VCs, who have done this thing many times before. So they tend to appoint an adviser, who is usually an accountant or solicitor. Advisers enjoy this sort of work because, frankly, it's a lot more interesting than audit or tax or drafting property leases.

Advisers are great for us, as they find deals and get the business plan in shape, but the downside is that they then put us in competition with other VCs and beat the shit out of us on terms. We try to even things up by finding deals ourselves and introducing these back to advisers but we do so through gritted teeth knowing they still won't hesitate to beat us up on terms, even though they owe the deal to us. We can also offer to buy lots of really expensive due diligence reports from them and hold out the prospect of introducing them to our extensive portfolio as a potential source of clients.

It never really feels comfortable, though. If you try to maintain equal relationships with every adviser you often end up disappointing all of them. This is also true in reverse: an adviser can introduce a deal to five VCs but only one can win the deal. So what usually happens is that, beneath the rhetoric, cliques form where a particular adviser works most often with a particular VC. The irony is that the management team then ends up suspicious that their own advisers might be more interested in maintaining their relationship with the VC than beating the shit out of them on their behalf.

Complex, isn't it?

Unfortunately Flagpole is out of the office and the Submission for P K Stationery is picked up by the awful Derek Sach who, true to his reputation, is about as pleasant as a pint of vinegar. He refuses to speak to me directly and instead communicates via Cicero, who is forced to do a shuttle negotiation up and down stairs. The first message is that the whole commercial proposition is deeply flawed and he won't approve it. However, when I add an extra 10% to our equity stake, he changes his mind and decides it's no longer deeply flawed and he will approve it after all. Funny that.

The deal completes and I am disappointed not to receive a complimentary box of delightful stationery. I do find myself wondering in the aftermath who had really made the decision to invest – me or the spreadsheet.

But I am comforted by that comment from the industrial adviser. There's no way *this* one is going to go bust within two weeks, is it? Despite his reassuring words, this time I really do feel scared. Whatever the official policy on witch hunts, if this one goes wrong, I can't guarantee I won't find myself being dunked in the village pond or burned at the stake.

Cicero asks me to look at a business plan that has been copied to us from London Office. It concerns a company called Maccess, which distributes automotive parts. The corporate owner wants to sell it and management have circulated a business plan to numerous private equity funds in order to secure finance for a management buyout. London doesn't really want to involve us but, since the company's headquarters are on our patch, for political reasons they have to be seen to 'get the input' from the local office.

Suspecting some kind of political stitch-up, I approach the business plan with some degree of scepticism. It's extremely professional and comprehensive, having been prepared by one of the big accounting firms, and there are pages and pages on the market positioning and operations and management history. Which is all great stuff, but what causes me to catch my breath is the size of the company: it has sales of £50m and is making profits of nearly £8m. In my world, those are huge numbers. The average size of MBO we are looking at in Birmingham is probably around £5m, but this company is probably going to sell for £40m or more. That could be £20m of cash out! Our average investment size at this time is probably £250k, although it's rising all the time. I honestly didn't know that 3i *did* deals of this size.

Except, apparently, we don't; I call the London Office controller handling the case, who promptly tells me he's already decided to bounce the deal.

I am astonished. I'm sure there will be plenty of issues and questions to ask about the business but it's obviously a real, proper company that is highly profitable. This guy should see some of the stuff I look at on a daily basis. Personally I would meet the management team, be extremely sycophantic in the hope of at least staying in the process long enough to propose some terms, and then shunt it off to Industry Department to see what they make of it.

'Well, the thing is,' he explains, 'that to achieve their forecasts management are going to have to achieve four things: add 10% to the top line; increase the gross margin by a couple of basis points; reduce overheads as a percentage of sales by a couple of basis points and tighten up working capital by a few basis points. Personally I can see them maybe achieving two of those things, but not all four.'

I feel like I'm gazing out of the windscreen into a sudden snow flurry of basis points. What even is a basis point? Anyway – really? I enquire as to which two things he considers unachievable. He says he doesn't know but I'm missing the point: he just thinks it's unlikely that management can achieve four things at once.

Saying no because management has to achieve four things at once. I add that one to my list. I decide to call it the *Animal Farm* principle: *two things good, four things bad.* Perhaps I should paint that up on the office wall for the benefit of the other farm animals.

When I share this experience with the team, they offer a different explanation. The London controller was just saving face. He knew there was no way Investment Committee would ever approve a deal of this size. 3i is terrified of doing big buyouts, fearing they are all hugely overpriced and just a very quick way to lose an awful lot of money.

Cicero, though, is undeterred by the apparent scepticism on the Tenth Floor over large deals. In his new 'market-facing' role he has brought in a large MBO, which he intends to lead himself. Luckily for me, he's asked me to work with him because of my experience with the Vauxhall car dealership and my having looked at the Maccess deal recently. He seems to enjoy being a dealer again; the wolfish smile is back on his face.

Charles Clark has a huge, national portfolio of car dealerships, including franchises for Vauxhall, Ford, Landrover and

BMW. It's headquartered in Birmingham and has come to us via one of the local advisers who is getting a name for himself arranging MBOs. There's a beauty parade and we've been given a chance to meet management. The business plan is very professional. To be honest, as I read it, I have my doubts about the investment opportunity; there's so little money to be made out of selling and servicing cars. But I suppose the fact that they have a variety of different franchises reduces the risk. And, even if your margins are wafer-thin, if you do a lot of sales you can still make a lot of profit. But there'll be time to worry about all that later – the important thing now is that there's a big deal going down on our patch and we're in on it.

The problem, though, is that this is a massive deal, right up there in the Premier Foods category. The adviser tells us that preliminary negotiations with the vendor indicate they are expecting offers in the region of £80m. Even if those numbers stack up commercially, it's far from obvious that the Tenth Floor will be willing to let us play with a deal of this size.

Cicero decides that we need London Office on board as allies and they send two executives up to Birmingham to accompany us to the initial management presentation. The London controllers dislike having to come to Birmingham and are sniffier than a couple of Victorian memsahibs on a tour of New Delhi. What captures my attention, though, is that they have laptop computers on which they have a financial model. I ask them for a copy but they tell me, haughtily, that regional controllers aren't to be trusted with it. In any case, they are using Lotus 1-2-3 which, as I discovered with P K Stationary, doesn't work on our system. I relay this to Cicero and see a flash of something in his eyes. He gets out his wallet, hands over his company credit card and tells me to go and buy a laptop. Fortunately, just off

Colmore Row is one of those early computer shops run by a couple of pale-skinned, pony-tailed geeks where the windows are piled up with unopened boxes of brand new computers and the interior is littered with software disks and unidentifiable cables with strange connectors on the end. So I pay it a visit and half an hour later I'm back, a posse of intrigued controllers surrounding my desk as I unpack a brand-new IBM laptop and load up Lotus 1-2-3 from a floppy disk. Having practiced with P K Stationery, it takes me only three days to write my very own MBO spreadsheet model and incorporate the Charles Clark forecasts into it.[17]

The spreadsheet model makes doing an MBO easy. You just plug in the management forecasts, enter your desired IRR of 30% in Goalseek, have a sip of tea while the numbers tumble across the page and whistle happily when the answer materialises in front of your eyes. No wonder London Office didn't want us to have it – this is deal pricing for the masses. The interesting thing is how easy it is to get to the indicated valuation of £80m. At that price the company's cashflow copes easily with the buyout loans and our dividends, and the returns look very attractive. No wonder everybody loves big MBOs, if this sort of profitability is typical.

When I send London a copy of my model – I have to send

---

17 You might be confused as to why I had to write a totally new spreadsheet model. The model for P K Stationery was used to manipulate the operational numbers of the business - sales, profits and cashflow - to get the overall funding requirement down. An MBO model just takes the operational cashflows and applies a financial structure to them. These financial structures can be quite complex, hence the need for a spreadsheet. If you're still confused, hang on in there. There's a fuller explanation of the smoke and mirrors of MBO financing – otherwise known as 'financial engineering' – in the next chapter *A Change in the Wind*.

a floppy disk down to them by Royal Mail – it is a good ten minutes before the spluttering on the other end of the phone stops. I am handed over to a London Local Director who, in the plumiest of Eton accents, rips into me for getting ideas above my station and demolishes, one by one, all the commercial assumptions in my model. Dutifully, I write down all his criticisms and incorporate them into the model. By the end of the day I am writing the Submission.

If we can pull this off it would be an astonishing coup. Our cash out would be £21m. – that's against an entire office cash out budget of just £30m for the year, and we're already two-thirds of the way there. We could possibly hit £50m, which is a sensational number. Much though I love the Tunnock's teacakes at Leek Dyeing & Finishing Company, this is a lot more fun.

The key is whether Investment Committee will approve it. The returns look very attractive but the fear is that they just don't want to risk that amount of money in any one deal.

It turns out there is indeed something wrong with P K Stationery and I now know what it is.

Everything.

The trouble with start-ups is that they are usually bad ideas that masquerade as great ideas right up to the point where they are confronted by reality. The worst thing you can do when assessing a start-up is to assume your intellect is an asset rather than a liability – like Socrates thought you could tell whether the earth went around the sun or vice versa by discussing it with a dumb conversational companion whilst strolling through an olive grove. Our intellectual vanity deceives us into believing we can assess all the many variables and process them into a

sound commercial judgement as to what will work and what
won't. You can't. The future is a complex and mysterious country
where things happen that you can never predict, no matter how
clever or experienced you are.

The shops are costing more to open than Neil allowed for.
Rents are higher than forecast. It is harder to find locations
than anticipated and the ones we have found aren't good ones.
Good store managers are scarce, the product costs more than
he budgeted for and he's overestimated what he can price the
product at. Within three months, the company has run out of
money.

In exasperation I ask, sarcastically, if anything is going right.

'Well, it's a good job I'm here.'

I squint at him. Oh my God, he's being serious!

There's a yawning chasm opening up under me. Why the
fuck won't these deals go right for me? Everyone else in the
office is doing deals and none of them seem to turn into instant
catastrophes. I had come to believe that Samji Industries was
an aberration caused by naivety and inexperience but now
it's happening all over again. While the situation with P K
Stationery is not yet fatal, the fact that it's gone awry already
is mortifying. An awful feeling starts to creep over me that I've
been born short of some 'right stuff' gene that is required for
making successful investments.

Neil's position is that I'm just being negative. This is
apparently the trouble with people like me. There is nothing
that another £100k and a further sprinkling of Neil magic pixie
dust can't sort out.

I send the industrial adviser back in and he suggests we
appoint a 'strong non-executive chairman'. I'm not at all sure
what a strong non-executive chairman looks like. Big biceps

and powerful thighs? I think it's something to do with being prepared to pick an argument with the managing director. How does that work then? If there is a disagreement between the two of them – and presumably the whole point is that the new chairman will have a different view than the MD – does being 'strong' mean that he gets his way? In which case, is the MD still the MD? Perhaps the idea is that a vigorous exchange of views will lead to a more 'robust' decision? It's all very confusing but I don't dare ask; the truth is, I've been using the phrase '*strong* chairman' myself for at least a couple of years so I can't exactly turn around now and admit I don't know what it means, can I? I do know that a strong chairman is different, in some subtle and mysterious way, from a *good* chairman but what that precise difference is eludes me for the present.

Anyway, not mine to reason why … I plunder our list of recommended non-executives and find somebody who has been a divisional managing director of a large high-street retailer. He reports that the concept is good but Neil is an arse and the whole strategy needs revisiting. He would, however, be prepared to take it on for a handsome salary and 5% of the equity. I am far from convinced he is the answer but appropriating 5% of Neil's equity and passing it over to someone who clearly has it in for him feels really, really good.

There is a spectacular night out involving the team, our Legal Department and a number of local advisers. A Greek restaurant is involved and we may have slightly overdone it with the plate smashing.

Several of us end up back at my house playing drinking games. When I wake up in the morning and come down to breakfast, there is a partner from one of Birmingham's leading legal firms fast asleep on my sofa in jacket, tie and underpants. How odd. Why did he take his trousers off but leave his jacket and tie on? I tiptoe out without disturbing him.

Later that day I find myself in a meeting with the same lawyer and his clients. He flushes slightly, but I don't say anything. On the other hand, it's truly extraordinary how many trouser-based metaphors you can come up with during the course of a single business meeting, if you really put your mind to it.

To general amazement, Investment Committee has approved our Charles Clark deal. I'm astonished to be honest, as they seem to be having one of their periodic seizures over the prospect of an imminent recession and are rejecting everything as too expensive. Cicero must have played a blinder. He's brilliant at politics. There's not much point in winning a beauty parade if you can't get it through Committee. I think it's the right decision, though, as the returns look very good.

We proudly submit a written proposal to the management team endorsing a bid up to a value of £80m, subject to due diligence, and confirming that our approvals are in place. The adviser tells us that a deadline has been set by the vendor for bids and he'll let us know the outcome in due course.

Predictably, Neil is not happy when I tell him we want to appoint a non-executive chairman. His claws come out and he hisses at me.

I try and reason with him. Things aren't going well, and he'll undoubtedly benefit from the experience and wise counsel of an experienced businessman. I show him the proposed chairman's

CV but he's unimpressed.

'Big company guy. Doesn't have the first clue about working in a small business.'

He also disagrees that things aren't going well. There are always setbacks in business.

It's obvious that I won't let it go, though, so he tries a different tack: he agrees in principle to the appointment of a chairman but he'll find a more appropriate one himself.

I may be inexperienced but I'm not daft. If I leave this to Neil, nothing will happen for three months and then he'll turn up with a mate from his golf club.

I'm beginning to lose my temper and in frustration rip a page out of the Clump playbook. 'Look, Neil … you need more money and the only place you're going to get it is from us. Now, I know you don't like it, but the bottom line is no chairman, no money. Now what's it to be?'

He presses his lips together in a thin line but his eyes flick down in a submissive gesture – I know I've got him. He'll take the money and he'll take the bloody chairman too.

On the way back to the office I realise I'm driving too fast. The truth is that felt good. It's only later, when the buzz dies down, that I realise what a risk I took. If he'd called my bluff I would have had to write off £250k.

Cicero calls me and asks me to come down to his office.

He's just taken a call from the adviser to the Charles Clark management. We haven't won the deal.

A small consolation is that we haven't lost to another venture capital firm. The seller has entered into an exclusivity arrangement with a trade buyer. The adviser assures us, though, how impressed the management team were with our proposal; had they succeeded in their bid, they would have chosen us as their lead investor. Then again, they're probably saying that to all the boys.

'There's something else,' says Cicero. 'We'd like you to move to Nottingham office. You'll be promoted to senior controller and go as number two to the Local Director, Dogfight. It's a great move and recognition of the work you've been doing here, particularly on Charles Clark.'

The news spreads fast, both about Charles Clark and my proposed move, and I have many visitors for the rest of the day. It's early evening before I get to tidy up the Charles Clark file for archiving. As I'm hole punching the Submission for inclusion in the file, I notice something curious. I feel a cold sweat creep up on me; there's something I suddenly need to check. I still have the IBM laptop on my desk so I boot it up and load my financial model.

The profit and loss account includes a line deducting Corporation Tax at 35% from pre-tax profits. Since the latter are something like £9m, the tax is a significant drain on cashflow: £3m a year. The tax is paid over to the Inland Revenue nine months after the company's year end, so there's a linked cell in the cashflow section that picks up the Corporation Tax number from the profit and loss account for the previous year and removes the equivalent amount from the cashflow.

Except, in my model, it doesn't. I've simply forgotten to put the formula into the cell and it's picking up nothing. The cashflow is wrong by £3m a year, a deficit that rises each year into the future as profits are forecast to grow.

No wonder the returns looked so bloody attractive! The error effectively wipes out £20m of debt over the life of the investment. To put it another way, I was effectively overvaluing the company by £20m. Actually, it might be even worse than that. I have to know. Wincing, I put the formula back in and watch as the figures in front of me transform from black to red and the attractive returns tumble to zero. At £80m, the company doesn't make enough profit to service the debt. The deal doesn't work: the company would have run out of cash. Sitting in the quiet of the office after everyone has gone home, the glow of attention from my Nottingham move has completely evaporated and my veins have turned to ice. I don't know what's luckier: that nobody noticed my error or that we didn't win the deal.

Gingerly, I put the Submission carefully in the file, seal it with a thick rubber band and, in big black indelible-marker ink, write on it, in a slightly shaky hand, the words TO BE ARCHIVED.

To be honest, I'm confused about the move to Nottingham. I really enjoyed working on the Charles Clark deal, despite the small, unfortunate, but happily immaterial oversight contained in the financial model, and I appreciate Cicero's positive remarks. I know I've done some decent things, but the inescapable truth is that I've only made two real investments: one was a disaster and the other is heading in the same direction, albeit not quite as fast. The question I'm asking myself is not whether I need a change of office but whether I need a change of job. I don't think I'm going to get fired but I'm facing the very real prospect of turning into a competent but undistinguished controller, doing modest numbers of solid but unremarkable growth capital deals and worthy portfolio work but not to be trusted with any real investments. It's childish, I know, but I don't *want* to be mediocre. I'm reluctant to give up and start looking for other jobs, but maybe there's something out there I would be better at. What that is, though, is not obvious. Some controllers leave to become finance directors of companies but that's not available to me as I'm not a qualified accountant. Some leave to take up advisory work, but that involves lots of networking, which I hate. I have a friend who works as a strategic consultant for McKinsey. That sounds more interesting, but he works rather too hard for my liking. And if I do decide to stick with venture capital, are my chances of coming good better with a fresh start in a new office or does that just add another layer of risk? If I am going to leave Birmingham, perhaps I'd be better off joining a competitor in London. All this stuff starts to churn around in my head but I don't want to discuss it with anyone for fear it will make me sound pitiable and self-indulgent.

Then somebody tells me there are five times as many women as men in Nottingham. Enough said. I tell Cicero that, sad though I will be to leave Birmingham, out of loyalty to the broader interests of 3i, I'm prepared to take a chance and accept the move.

It's a bittersweet moment, leaving Birmingham. I've come to like the place. I've learned a lot and made lots of friends. But has it been a personal success? For the financial year ending March 1989, we beat our £30m cash out target and I contributed about £1.5m to that, except that £1m was just a loan to a firm of accountants and £250k was into P K Stationery, which is already in trouble. There were a few other loans to portfolio cases and I also supported some of the other controllers on management buyouts, including Cicero on Charles Clark. But, both in Birmingham and around the country, the market is booming and other people are doing real deals, big deals, successful deals.

The reality is that my breakthrough deal feels as far away as ever. Perhaps it's never going to come.

7

A CHANGE IN THE WIND

'Leverage, says you. I think I feel a change
in the wind, says I.'

Pirates of the Caribbean: The Curse of the Black Pearl

May 1989 to June 1990
In the end it turns on two words and a question mark.

I transfer over to Nottingham office on 1st May 1989 and
by 30th June I have completed £8m of cash out and completed
not one but two proper management buyouts. You could say
it's a good start.

We receive an approach from an adviser with an interesting
deal. And a problem. Fitchett & Woollacott and Whitmore's
Timber are two separate companies being sold by the same
parent company. Fitchett is a timber merchant and Whitmore's
sources, treats and sells oak for the building trade. They are both
profitable, well-managed companies with reasonable growth

167

prospects. One of our competitors, CinVen[18], had been working on a deal to back two simultaneous MBOs but has pulled out at the last minute, deciding the agreed price is too high. In desperation, the management adviser has contacted us to see if we are prepared to step into CinVen's shoes and complete the deal. I meet both management teams, visit the companies and have no doubt that – at the right price and given sufficient time – these are deals we would be willing to do.

The vendor is having a difficult year and wants these two businesses off its balance sheet by its financial year end. The problem is that the vendor's year end is just two weeks away. On my way back from the company I drop into Dogfight's office and tell him about the situation. I explain that I think there's a good investment opportunity here but there is no way we could investigate, negotiate and complete a deal – particularly one involving *two* companies – in just two weeks.

Where Cicero was smooth and infinitely calculating, Dogfight is about as subtle as a charging rhinoceros. Cicero liked to think his way around objections, test boundaries and examine assumptions. Dogfight just drives straight over them. Cicero would have helped me analyse the problem, and suggested I explore whether there was any way the deadline could be extended. I could imagine his hands tidying the problem into a more manageable corner. Dogfight just says:

'Why not?'

'What?'

'Why can't you get the deal done in two weeks?'

There are a dozen reasons. We have to get an industrial

---

18 The venture capital arm of the British Coal Pension Fund.

adviser in, negotiate a deal with management, arrange banking, obtain Investment Committee approval, complete all our due diligence and negotiate a whole set of investment documentation. Since, although it's one purchase, it's being done as two separate MBOs, we would have to do all this in duplicate and in parallel. It is impossible.

We do it in thirteen days.

And the quid pro quo is that we get £2m off the price.

The 3i Nottingham team occupy an elegant converted townhouse, perched on a cliff overlooking Nottingham Castle. The interior has been greatly modified, most notably by driving a spiral staircase right up the centre of the house like a corkscrew driven up through a cork. Where Colmore Row had been wide and squat, the Ropewalk is thin and tall, extending up four floors with a tiny crow's nest of an office at the top, furnished with a desk and a chair but kept vacant. The whole arrangement rather reminds me of one of my favourite childhood books, *The Magic Faraway Tree*: one winds one's way up through the floors via the spiral trunk, passing little hideaways inhabited by different characters. On the ground floor are two secretaries (again, usually referred to as 'the girls'), who also act as receptionists, and a single meeting room. Dogfight occupies an office on the first floor – with a bay window and a magnificent view over the castle – in which there is also a large meeting room table. Where Cicero was a sofa man, Dogfight is definitely a meeting table man. My privileged position as the most senior controller entitles me to an office of my own next to Dogfight's. One further circuit up the spiral staircase takes you into the main office, capable of accommodating two or three further controllers but presently only occupied by two: Chris and Bernard. There is another office on that floor, occupied by Clive, a senior controller who joined at the same time as me and who I know from the training courses. Unlike Birmingham, there is no split between New Business and Portfolio; we are expected to fulfil both roles.

Relative to Birmingham office, it's a small team and a small market. It would be a good year for Nottingham if we did twenty deals and £10m-£15m of cash out.

On the plus side, I am much more fluent now in the vocabulary of investment and have a good working knowledge of how to get deals through the system. The move to Nottingham means there is no more senior controller to divert incoming deals away from me. In short, I am fully equipped to deliver, provided I can actually find deals worthy of building a reputation on. Going to a smaller market, without the dense web of advisers and industrial hinterland that existed in the West Midlands, is my biggest concern.

The phrase 'Why not?' changes all that. Two words and a question mark. It is the champagne bottle that launches the ship.

On the other hand, despite feeling very pleased with myself, there's still a claw of self-doubt gripping my insides. It's all very well launching the ship; what matters is what happens when it hits the water. If this one sinks, it's going to be hard to resist the conclusion that I'm essentially just a fool, too easily parted from someone else's money.

With relatively few active advisers in Nottingham, we have to find the deals ourselves. This means the dreadful spectre of cold calling.

Cold calling is admired and encouraged by everyone who

doesn't actually have to do it. The Tenth Floor loves the idea that we are a deal-originating machine, using our extensive regional network and the sheer weight of numbers to access deals that our competitors will only learn of when they read about them in the newspapers. They are also convinced that, because we are getting to these deals first and (so they believe) exclusively, we are able to get better terms by way of higher equity stakes or lower entry valuations.

It's a lovely narrative but, like an old-fashioned reel of camera film, it spoils pretty quickly when exposed to sunlight. In my experience cold calling is an unpleasant, unproductive activity that rarely succeeds in anything other than wasting valuable time, irritating the unwelcoming targets and embarrassing the poor controller who is obliged to do it. In any case, even if you do arrive at a deal before the competition, all that happens is that management appoint an adviser anyway, whose first step is to bring in other venture capitalists to compete with you. But since when did anyone high up in an organisation allow reality to inconvenience a pleasing theory?

The first problem with cold calling is who to call. There are lots of corporate databases you can trawl, many of them derived from records at Companies House. But, frankly, you might as well pick up the telephone directory, choose a page and dial at random. The second problem is getting through to the managing director, who will be vigorously defended by a switchboard and a personal assistant whose precise purpose is to stop people like you getting through and wasting the man's valuable time. Indeed, the vast majority of cold calls wither faster than testicles dunked in icy water when confronted with the question: 'Will he know what it's about?' Some of the more inventive controllers, in an attempt to circumvent this humiliating fate, pretend they are calling from the police about a break in at home, or their children's school about an outbreak of meningitis, but this involves the obvious risk of incurring the object's wrath once the deception is exposed, as it must be.

For my part, I discover a simple and effective strategy for cold calling that evades all of these problems, and saves enormous amounts of time to boot, in one simple stroke.

I just don't do it.

Except the once.

I have the local Nottingham newspaper on my desk and happen to be reading about a company called Nottingham Group, which has recently opened a new warehouse facility. It is exactly the sort of situation where we are encouraged to cold call. The warehouse must have cost money and has maybe given rise to a growth capital opportunity. And I need examples of cold calling that I can put on my appraisal to show I have actually done some. Usually it's safe enough to just make them up, but it would be better if I could name a real company. And I am bored, as things are very quiet. All the same, there's a little part of me groaning at the prospect of having to make the call and I manage to prevaricate most of the day, finding an infinite number of excuses to put it off. Finally, at about six in the evening, reasoning that by now everyone has probably gone home anyway, I dial the number I have lifted from the telephone directory. After two rings, a man's voice announces that I have reached Nottingham Group.

'Could I speak to the managing director, please?'

'My name is David Mansfield. I am the managing director. How can I help?'

That throws me. I do the only thing that comes to mind in the moment. I babble: something about 3i and growth capital and the new warehouse and the possibility of a meeting.

There is a long pause.

'Actually, your timing is impeccable. Why don't you come and see me first thing tomorrow morning? It would be best if you came before the staff arrive – could you be here at 6:30?'

Oh. Okay.

I'm seized with a creeping depression. It looks like my worst fears are being realised.

Six months on and Whitmore's Timber is trading well above budget, which is a truly satisfying feeling. That's the good news. But Fitchett, which is by far the larger company, is trading way behind its budgets. Okay, it's still making profits and there's no immediate cash crisis, but the signs aren't good. I've learned already that the first management accounts to appear after a deal has been completed are a big indicator of how things will go. Above budget almost certainly means the forecasts were conservative; if they are below budget, that's probably because management were inflating the prospects in order to get the deal away. Moreover, the word from Birmingham is that P K Stationery is still struggling and has had to be refinanced – again.

I'm getting that empty feeling of helplessness. Every time I do a proper equity investment it goes wrong. What's wrong with me? It's all very well getting deals done but how the fuck are you supposed to tell which ones are actually going to make money?

3i talks about 'commercial judgement': the ability to spot a good investment opportunity. But is commercial judgement a talent? A gift? Something you're born with? Or is it something that can be learned, acquired with experience? The way it's talked about in 3i rather suggests the former. Commercial judgement is to 3i what 'divine grace' is to the Catholic Church – an enigmatic but precious quality that is indefinable, except you know it when you see it. Controllers are not necessarily required to display commercial judgement – our primary role is just to find the deals – but you won't climb the hierarchy without it. You don't have to possess divine grace to help out at church with the catering, but it's pretty essential if you want to make Pope.

What *is* commercial judgement and what *does* it look like when you see it? I spend some time thinking about this.

In the basement of the office there are archives where all the old files are kept. I decide to do some research and spend some time browsing old and new files, trying to find some lessons in what makes a successful investment. My methodology is to look up the original Submissions and file memos from the time of the initial investment and compare what the original controller thought was going to happen with what actually did happen. Since the files go back at least thirty years, there's a good spread of cases; some have done well, some have done badly and there are a lot that just drifted into a twilight zone where they neither succeeded nor failed. The land of the living dead is well populated.

I've been a professional venture capitalist nearly five years now, been promoted to a reasonably senior investment grade, been on numerous training courses and I'm only just doing this now! On the other hand, it definitely beats cold calling.

What emerges from this little personal research project is that there is a very low correlation between what we expect of an investment when we make it and what happens subsequently. I find myself reading articulate, confident, closely argued Submissions and then reading the subsequent case file. The two simply don't match up.

Investments that go wrong invariably go wrong for reasons that we fail to anticipate – but, then again, investments often go right for reasons that we also don't anticipate. We spend a lot of time debating forecasts but the evidence seems to be that most management forecasts are about as accurate as a paper dart thrown into a force nine gale. All the work that goes into describing and analysing the business, assessing the forecasts, discussing and negotiating the valuation – it certainly makes us feel good about ourselves but it doesn't actually make our investment decisions any better.[19]

There are a few well-known names on some of the old Submissions, controllers who have now become elevated to the most senior ranks. I can't help but notice there is no evidence that these individuals were any better at anticipating investment outcomes than anyone else. For some reason I find that a grimly pleasing insight.

This apparent randomness about investment outcomes is both disturbing and weirdly liberating. If our best efforts make no difference, then what is the point of us? On the other hand, the prospect of a sudden organisational enlightenment that we are all totally useless seems comfortingly remote. We may all be imposters but, if so, we're very well-paid imposters and the chances of us being rumbled any time soon seem pretty low.

---

19 Thirty years later, I discover there is actually a name for this! Validity bias. Because some activity feels useful, we are prone to believe that it is. Don't get me started on how endemic validity bias is in the investment industry.

3i MEMORANDUM

From: **Paul Traynor**
To: **File**
Date: **8th March 1990**
Subject: **Nottingham Group**

Following a cold call, I visited this company for an early morning meeting and met managing director, David Mansfield.

Nottingham Group is the UK's leading supplier of educational material to schools, which it does through the publication of a mail order catalogue that is distributed to pretty much every school and educational establishment in the country. There are several thousand products, ranging from basic items such as consumables (pens/rulers/chalk etc.) to equipment (blackboards/chairs/desks/sports equipment). The company also has a smaller medical supplies division – again through a mail order catalogue – which goes to hospitals, GP surgeries, clinics etc. and supplies pretty much anything that doesn't require clinical certification: things like walking frames or disability aids. The company's head office in Nottingham is co-located with a new 100,000 square foot warehouse that receives, picks and despatches orders. Group turnover for the year to December 1989 was £26m and operating profit £1.9m.

The company is presently a subsidiary of Coats Viyella plc, the quoted textiles group, and indeed the origins of Nottingham Group are in selling fabrics to school craft departments but that represents only a tiny part of the business now.

NG has a market share of about 20% and there are a number

of competitors, of which the largest is E J Arnold with a share of about 15%, which is based in Leeds and owned by Robert Maxwell's Pergamon Press. David Mansfield has been in negotiation with Pergamon to acquire E J Arnold, which would have two benefits: the Leeds warehouse operation could be shut down and transferred into Nottingham (which has the capacity to absorb it) thereby eliminating one entire set of overheads, while at the same time the two product ranges could be consolidated to eliminate duplicates and to obtain greater volume discounts from suppliers, thus improving margins. However, when David put his acquisition proposal to the Coats Viyella Board it was rejected on the basis that it makes little sense to invest capital outside Coats' core business area, which is textiles. The rejection seems further to have triggered off a process of reflection by the board, leading to a decision to put Nottingham Group up for sale. David was informed of this decision the day prior to my visit. He was keen to meet me to establish whether it might be possible for management to make an offer for the business.

Whilst Coats has yet to establish a sale process, David understands that they intend to appoint advisers and to market the business widely to trade buyers, of which there are likely to be quite a number.

I confirmed to David that a buyout looked eminently feasible and we would be extremely keen to work with him and his team as lead investor. We talked through some of the issues regarding process, particularly how he manages the conflict between his responsibility to sell the business on behalf of the parent whilst also being a potential buyer. He was also inquisitive about 3i's track record in MBOs and our credentials as a potential lead investor.

Whilst David's priority is to bid for Nottingham Group itself, he was also curious whether it would be possible, at the same time, to continue with the acquisition of E J Arnold, in other words to acquire the two companies simultaneously as part of the same transaction. My response was that I couldn't see why not in principle, although it would obviously add another layer of complexity to the process.

Though it was only a fairly brief first meeting, I was extremely impressed by David Mansfield. He comes across as assured and knowledgeable, with good strategic vision and an impressive grasp of the details.

The first thing I notice about Nottingham Group is the car park. It's huge, covered in a beautifully smooth layer of immaculate tarmac, and it all belongs to Nottingham Group. This isn't a sub-contract engineering business in a shed on a shared industrial estate; this is a proper company. There's a very large and modern looking warehouse and a suite of modern offices, which have an electronic sliding door and a real reception area, with a receptionist's desk and a waiting area that even has a coffee machine. To be honest I'm a bit blindsided – cold calls don't deliver meetings with proper companies.

There's no one in reception because dawn is still just breaking, but David must have been watching out for me as he appears in reception and lets me in. He leads me through silent corridors to his office, stopping on the way to make us both a cup of tea. He explains that he wanted to meet early, before the staff get in, because it's early days and he doesn't want rumours flying around. I can feel some big-game tension tightening across my chest. Everything is circumstantial so far, but there is a strong feeling that my reluctant cold call has led me to something quite unexpectedly significant. David is a neat man in his mid-forties. I would later learn he had been a semi-professional footballer in his youth. He is pleasant, civil, with an air of quiet authority.

We exchange some conversation and I can sense him cautiously checking me out. He asks a little about me and about 3i, and I think I must have passed his test because he switches to the purpose of the meeting and explains the situation concisely. He also shows me some abbreviated financial statements that serve to confirm that this is a proper company. He wants to know if I think it might be possible to do a management buyout. He says he expects I'll need to think it over and discuss it back at the office, but I say I don't need to think it over: clearly it's not only feasible but totally exciting too, and he'd be mad to let the opportunity go by and I would love to work with them to put the deal together. I think he's a little surprised how gushingly enthusiastic I am but he seems to appreciate it. We move on to the situation with E J Arnold and he's curious as to whether they might be able to combine both deals and acquire Arnold simultaneously, or would that be a step too far? Could it be done?

This is a big, complex transaction for me and I'm suffering vertigo, feeling like a ten-year-old standing on the edge of a cliff, being dared to jump into the sea. Do I jump, or back away and do the sensible thing, which is to pass it on to someone better equipped to deal with it?

There's also the question of whether I could ever hope to get this approved. I'm well aware of 3i's scepticism regarding large deals and it would be excruciatingly embarrassing to start running with this only to be brought up short by a withering denunciation from Dogfight or Flagpole. Or, should it ever get that far, Investment Committee itself.

Fuck it. I take a deep breath and jump.

'Why not?' I hear myself say.

The offices are starting to fill up and David no longer seems so concerned about keeping my presence invisible. He introduces me to his secretary and gives me a tour of the warehouse, which is just coming to life with the morning shift. I watch as staff in overalls, working from pick notes, push trolleys to the relevant shelf location, pull out the desired item, and move on, assembling the rest of the order. It all looks reassuringly calm, organised and efficient. I also notice the way everybody knows David and greets him informally and in a friendly way. That seems like a very good sign.

'I don't have to involve London Office, do I?'

Dogfight guffaws. 'London Office? That's like asking the groom if he needs a eunuch to help out with the bride on the wedding night.'

I have to think that one through for a minute. Then I get it. 'So that's a no, then?'

'Yes, Paul, that's a no. You just get on and win the deal and I'll sort out all the internal stuff.'

My hero.

With my new zeal for doing deals that are profitable – as opposed to just doing deals – I go through the Nottingham Group forecasts in a level of detail I have never even dreamed of before. I ask every question I can think of and challenge everything. David answers every single question assuredly and persuasively. I can't fault him on anything. I feel like a British general at the Somme, sending my questions over the top in waves only for them to be clinically slaughtered by the steady tack-tack of David's replies. At the end of the day, there are dead questions strewn all over the desk but I'm not sure I've really advanced very far. All I have is a list of detailed assumptions that I know to be entirely reasonable and well thought through. That doesn't necessarily mean they are achievable. I lob a last air-burst shell towards the enemy trench, more in hope than expectation.

'So what do *you* think David? Will you achieve these forecasts?' He smiles and shrugs his shoulders. 'They're just forecasts.'

I can see why industrial advisers always say forecasts are 'ambitious'. They don't know any better than I do. They are just covering their arses. Nobody knows. Forecasts are just forecasts.

I like David more and more, and we seem to get on well, but he's not going to give me the deal because I happened to make a well-timed phone call. We're in competition. Competing for large MBOs is sexy though – as long as you win.

He's invited us and two other London-based venture capitalists to a beauty parade.

What a strange thing to call it: are we expected to put on swimsuits and a brightly coloured sash with our company name on it? Do we strut up a catwalk towards a man with a microphone and say 'world peace, children and saving the environment' when we're asked a question? Does the winner get a crown and appear on the front of *Hello* magazine?

I've put on a bit of weight recently. I hope that's not going to count against me. I bet the London competition will be wearing expensive Italian suits – maybe it's time to trade up on my M&S pinstripe.

It turns out that a beauty parade is just a normal meeting, where you get the floor in order to sell yourself and your firm to management. Apparently, the trick is to make a presentation on the 'soft factors', like how great you are to work with, and then present your detailed financial proposal. It actually sounds like fun. I do, however, take the precaution of buying a terrifyingly expensive new suit for the occasion, although I rather spoil the effect by dribbling coffee onto my tie during the first, nervous opening moments of the meeting.

3i has this marketing strapline about being long-term and hands-off. It's designed to emphasise that we're different and more wholesome than those fickle short-term city investors, and to reassure managers that we'll fully respect their managerial autonomy and independence. It's a message that has evolved to calm the anxieties of SME owners who have no experience working with a professional investor. Naturally, I incorporate all the long-term/hands-off bollocks into my presentation but I can tell David and his team are just waiting politely for me to get to the interesting part. Management teams doing buyouts don't really care about long-term or hands-off. They're perfectly happy for you to nag them all the way to 'GO' on the first circuit of the Monopoly board if it means they get to collect their millions. So 'long-term and hands-off' is not going to win you any beauty parades, but we're always careful to say in a submission that it's what won us the deal. Investment Committee likes that.

Management teams contemplating a buyout have a really simple checklist of things they are looking for in a lead venture capitalist. First, they want to know that you actually have money to invest: basic, boring, but kind of critical. Second, they want to know that you know how to organise a buyout, which is most easily tested by asking if you've done one before.

After that we get into the thick of the action. The real purpose of a beauty parade is to drive the best terms out of you; this is done by getting you to table your proposal so it can be compared to what your competitors are offering. Most management teams like to say that money isn't everything, but they're lying. It is. If you doubt that, get a really companionable, sincere, trustworthy guy to offer management 40% of the equity, then a nasty, grasping, thoroughly duplicitous bastard to offer 45%, and see which one they choose. To be honest, I would be the same. If my company might be worth £75m-£100m in five years' time, that 5% could be an extra £5m. Most of us, including me, would happily work with Genghis Khan for that sort of money.

Even more important is how much the management can afford to bid for the business. The vendor, in this case Coats Viyella, might make all sorts of warm noises about preferring management to win but that's not going to stop them touting the business around widely to alternative buyers and accepting the highest offer. In these early days, MBO bids are generally met with scepticism: how can a management team expect to compete with the 'synergies' – the opportunity to increase profits by merging the two companies – available to a trade buyer?[20] By definition, the management team have no such synergies available to them and the size of their offer is restricted by what the available cashflow can support. Commercial logic therefore dictates that a trade buyer will almost always be expected to

___

20 How times have changed! In the present day the first names on any seller's list are private equity firms, who are considered much more likely to pay an elevated price compared to a trade buyer.

offer more than a management team. Where vendors are naïve, though, is in failing to understand how management teams can influence the process by playing down the prospects when talking to trade bidders and playing them up to venture capitalists. It is completely normal for one set of forecasts to be sent out to trade bidders while a different, more ambitious, set is circulated to VCs. More subtly, the management team can play down the quality of the business and the achievability of the forecasts when they meet the trade buyers. Even a raised eyebrow here, or an inflexion of the voice there, can suggest the forecast is just a tad too ambitious. So in practice, the playing field is perhaps more level than it might have appeared. But still, management must put down a number that will at least match, and ideally beat, the bids from trade buyers. It's all very well offering the management a large slice of equity, but it counts for nothing if you don't beat the trade. 25% of nothing is nothing.

So the purpose of a beauty parade is to demonstrate that we have the money and know what we are doing, and for us to table two numbers: the maximum offer the team can make to Coats Viyella, and how much equity we are proposing to give to David and the team.

Strangely enough, 3i actually looks quite good to the Nottingham Group management team at this point. We have a massive balance sheet – at least £3bn – and do more deals than the bling department on the Shopping Channel. The fact that the vast majority of them are £250k growth capital investments is not something to which I intend to draw the team's attention just yet. Plus, our corporate logo in pastel shades looks very pretty on an overhead projector. But I'm anxious about what's going to happen when this gets to Committee, although not too long ago they did approve the £80m buyout of Charles Clark, and this to me is a much better deal.

Somehow, though, a little voice in my head keeps telling me it doesn't quite work like that …

On my promotion to senior controller, I'm allowed an upgrade under the Company Car Policy. This is very exciting.

Very little is more important to the 3i controller than his company car and accordingly the car policy is a source of constant discussion, complaint and resentment. The basic problem is that all the young controllers want a hot hatchback – ideally the Volkswagen Golf GTi or an Escort XR3i – but this is deemed inappropriate by whoever sets the car policy. There seems to be a management obsession about how it looks when we turn up to a customer in a hot hatch. Obviously the Tenth Floor is under the impression that our customers like to sit testily and judgementally at their office window when expecting a visit from their 3i controller, like a watchful old guard dog waiting for the postman to open the garden gate. This strikes us as unlikely.

Deprived of the opportunity to obtain a hot hatchback, I select a Montego Turbo. It is a truly dreadful car with a trashy spoiler on the boot and a marked tendency for bits, both interior and exterior, to drop off spontaneously. On the other hand, it goes like shit off a shovel. Unfortunately this feature also makes it popular with a less scrupulous demographic element and it is stolen twice from outside my flat. The policeman who comes round to take the details is deeply disapproving and says neither he nor any of his colleagues would ever drive a car like that. I expect that's because he disapproves of the temptation to drive dangerously and at high speed.

'No' he says. 'Because it would just get nicked all the time.'

There's a girl I've met who mistakes the Montego for a BMW: she tells me she considers BMWs to be a sign of wealth and maturity, which I decide to interpret as a roundabout way of saying she's open to a date if I ask politely. Fortunately for me, the Montego gets stolen for use in an armed robbery before she realises her error and, cleverly, I order a BMW in time for the first date. She completely fails to notice the change of make but picks up that my car is now a different colour. I tell her I had to have it resprayed after it was in an accident.

What was that about honesty being the best policy?

On my new portfolio is a company called Tecquipment. Tecquipment is, without a shadow of doubt, a brilliant company. It designs, manufactures and supplies all sorts of technical and scientific equipment for universities, science labs and schools. A frequent winner of the Queen's Award for Export, it is highly profitable and valuable and exactly the sort of company that deserves the benefit of our capital, not to mention our distinctive blend of financial and commercial skills.

The company arranges a meeting with me to let me know they have the opportunity to win a major contract to supply the entire university sector in Turkey, but it will require significant working capital, which they are looking to 3i to provide. It takes me half a heartbeat to say yes. This is exactly what 3i was put on this planet to do.

Except, apparently not. My Submission is rejected by Investment Committee. Of course, I'm not invited to the meeting and neither is Dogfight so we have no idea what their problem is and Flagpole is not much help either. He just makes vague noises about a 'gloomy economic outlook', 'step too far', 'political risk' and 'currency factors'. I make the mistake of taking him at face value and go back to the befuddled management team. We spend several hours trying to decipher what IC might really be fretting about and devise a comprehensive rebuttal to all of the potential issues. I also – suspecting this is IC's usual shameful trick of demanding an improvement in terms by the back door – negotiate an extra 5% of the equity, completely rewrite the Submission to include the new arguments and put the deal back to Committee. It's rejected again and for the first time I lose my rag, forget my place and rant at Flagpole.

'Sorry, Paul, but they just don't like it.'

I go all Basil Fawlty. It's not my finest moment. 'They don't like it? *They don't like it?* **THEY DON'T LIKE IT?** What sort of a reason is that, for Christ's sake? This is a growth capital investment for a genuinely world-class company in which we've been a shareholder for the last ten years! If we're not prepared to do *this* then what *are* we prepared to do? If there's a genuine commercial objection then the very least we owe the management is to tell them what it is. You can't seriously expect me to go back to them and say we've turned it down because we *just don't like it!* How does that make us look? How does that make *me* look?'

By the time I reach the end of this tirade my voice has risen to a squeak. I sound like a toy rubber duck. I don't imagine it's the most intimidating conversation Flagpole has ever had.

You have to admire the way he handles it, though. Flagpole doesn't try and argue. He knows there's no way to justify this nonsense and pretending is only going to make things worse. He doesn't pull rank either. His technique is much more effective than that: he just stops talking.

You can't punch silence. My fury steams down the telephone

and evaporates pointlessly to atmosphere at the other end. He doesn't apologise, or hang up, or try to offer advice on how to handle the horrible communication I'm about to have with the Tecquipment management. He just waits me out.

Afterwards, I call the management team to deliver the news. I have never felt more ashamed in all my life.

Luckily I hear later that they've found a bank to provide the money. I'm astonished, and even more ashamed, that a bank is prepared to back them when their own shareholder wouldn't. It's not just a question of loyalty; there's no obvious security for the bank to take and they must be relying heavily on the cashflow kicking up sufficiently to cover the interest and repayments. It doesn't look like a banking deal at all. Intrigued, I ask which bank and am given an introduction to John Bell at Royal Bank of Scotland. He's a short man, ridiculously extroverted for a banker, and he's just taken over the Nottingham branch. He's very keen to do more work with us. Great, I say. If anything comes up, I'll let you know.

Generating an MBO proposal is a bit like assembling a flat-pack bookshelf from Ikea. You start by spreading all the parts out on the floor: senior debt, mezzanine debt,[21] preference shares, the amount management are going to invest personally, and of course the outrageous fees plundered by all the above plus a

---

21 Funny stuff, mezzanine debt. As the name suggests, it's a loan but one that ranks behind the senior debt and is therefore considered a lot riskier. To compensate for this additional risk, the lender imposes a high interest rate and takes equity in the company as well, usually in the form of options. In other words it's sub-prime lending under a different name. All the same, there are several specialist funds that have made a very large amount of money from providing mezzanine debt to the buyout sector.

wagon train of accountants, solicitors and other professionals. It's your job to assemble all this into a sturdy financial structure that can survive the bumps of active use for at least five to seven years.

Stitching this lot together is a process of iteration, like turning a kaleidoscope of numbers to get the image that suits you. You twist: the numbers tumble. You twist again, and the numbers tumble into a different pattern. You have to keep twisting until the pattern looks just right. This is why a spreadsheet is so important; it can twist and tumble thousands of times faster than you can and it doesn't make basic arithmetic errors. It's the smartest bit of kit ever – and the dumbest. If, for example, you were simply to forget to enter the appropriate formula in the cell for corporation tax, it won't warn you. Like any robot, it just keeps heading remorselessly in the direction of the cliff to which you've unwittingly pointed it.

The way an MBO financial structure works is like embarking and disembarking passengers onto an aircraft. Each lender or investor arrives with a particular suitcase full of cash, which is deposited with the crew (the management team), and then has to be ushered in the right order into the right seat: senior debt providers fill up the seats at the back, mezzanine fill up those in the middle, and equity investors sit in business class (of course). The magic happens while you're in the air, as the amount of money in the hold trebles or quadruples in value so that, when the flight is over and you collect your suitcase, it will contain considerably more cash than it did when you checked in. However, you have to disembark in strict reverse order: senior debt first, mezzanine second, then preference shares and finally the equity (investors and management together) which is entitled to everything that's left once the prior passengers have taken their allotted share. If things haven't gone well and the money hasn't multiplied, the last people off the plane go home with an empty suitcase rather than a full one. And, in the event of a fire on take-off, not everybody is going to make it out alive. So, before you embark, you spend a lot of time with the lawyers drafting up a complex set of agreements that legislate what happens in the unlikely (erm, actually not *that* unlikely) event of an accident: who gets to survive and who gets incinerated in the burning fuselage. In theory the captain (aka the CEO) is supposed to be brave and go down with the plane but in practice is very often caught shoving the women and children aside to save his own skin. That's capitalism.

There are lots of conventions as to the way deals are structured but I have no idea where they come from. Why does the senior debt have to be repaid in seven years rather than ten? Why not five? Why is the target IRR 30%? Why do we assume an exit in Year 5 on an earnings multiple of eight? Why are the management team expected to invest the equivalent of one year's gross salary? I don't know and perhaps nobody does. It's like one of those family rituals for who sits where at the dinner table; there probably was an explanation once but it's been lost long ago in the mists of time. Woe betide anybody who sits in Dad's place, though.

I plug the Nottingham Group forecasts into the financial model and iterate away until the vital numbers emerge: management can afford to offer £32m for Nottingham Group and Arnold combined and we can afford to give them 40% of the equity.

When I present these numbers at the beauty parade, David says we need to increase the management equity to match the other offers. He's a bloody good negotiator and I can't tell whether our offer is really inferior to our competitors or he's playing me, but I can't afford to take the chance. I propose a ratchet, which is a mechanism by which management can increase their equity percentage to 51% if they outperform their forecasts.

It's 4p.m. on a Friday when David calls to say they have decided to appoint 3i as their lead investor. The exhilaration is like rocket fuel injected straight into my veins and ignited. This is a feeling to which I could easily get addicted. I feel like I've won the World Cup and go on a huge bender with some mates.

When I wake up the next morning, there is plenty of residual euphoria but beneath my hangover is a niggly little question: how did I win that? My heart wants to say they really liked me on a personal level, while my head says we probably just gave them the highest equity percentage.

This is negative, unhelpful thinking and not conducive to my mental well-being. On reflection, I decide they probably just liked our long-term, hands-off philosophy.

Arranging finance for an MBO is like a pyramid of bullying.

At the top, the vendor approaches half a dozen potential buyers, narrows it down to two or three and bullies them into producing their best offer.

The management team approaches half a dozen venture capitalists, narrows them down to two or three and bullies them into producing their best offer.

The lead venture capitalist approaches half a dozen banks, narrows it down to two or three and bullies them into producing their best offer.

By the time your turn comes around to be the bully, you're

totally ready to give some back.

NatWest are the recognised leading bank in large MBOs, and a whole team comes up from London to pitch to me and the management team. It's like Goldilocks: there's a big banker, a medium banker and a spotty baby banker who says nothing but takes lots of notes. We sit through an interminable presentation on the bank's internal organisational structure and then get to the important part: their offer. It's very professionally set out with a document listing every conceivable term and condition, of which there are an awful lot. I am intrigued by a whole set of financial ratios the company is required to comply with or be 'in breach'. Being 'in breach' is nothing to do with a difficult birth; rather, it refers to an 'event of default' which is apparently a very, very bad thing that brings forth fire, pestilence, plague, swarms of locusts and the Four Horsemen of the Apocalypse. These ratios are apparently called 'covenants' – a new term to me that I initially misread, no doubt as a legacy of my Catholic upbringing, as 'convents'. For a few moments, the little black figures on the white page look like dancing nuns.

We need to give NatWest some competition, though. I remember my conversation with John Bell at the Royal Bank of Scotland and give him a call. It's a very long shot as, despite his helpfulness on Tecquipment, this is a very serious deal. This MBO will require a £20m term loan to finance two simultaneous acquisitions plus an additional working capital facility of £6m, all of which will have to be regulated by a set of agreements between the bank, the mezzanine provider and the equity syndicate. One shouldn't prejudge these things, but RBS are unlikely to be the front runner.

John is a cheery chap, though, with a refreshingly positive outlook on everything. He turns up to the meeting with just his assistant manager and no presentation on the bank's internal organisation chart. He just wants to know how he can help.

David has sent him the forecasts beforehand but I'm pretty sure John hasn't read them.

'Just remind me how much you're looking for,' John says.

David tells him.

John says he's sure that will be fine.

'Great,' says David, 'what interest rate will the bank want?'

'What are the other banks offering?' asks John.

'1.75% over Bank Base.'

'We'll do it for 1.5% then.'

'Okay! And what sort of covenants do you think the bank will be seeking?'

'What's a covenant?' asks John.

I hand him a photocopy of the NatWest sheet with the dancing nuns. He glances at it and says that looks fine.

After the bankers have left we are all agreed that NatWest were by far the most impressive and professional outfit. So I call John to tell him he's won the deal. The only issue is whether he can get it approved by his credit committee. We can't 'switch off' NatWest until we know that RBS can definitely deliver. 'Oh no problem,' John says. And he's not lying. Within a week we have an approved banking deal.

I think it's at that moment that I know the Royal Bank of Scotland is one day going to lead the civilised world down into a very deep, very dark hole.

You work hard on a deal, get to know the business, form a rapport with the management team, get agreement on price and equity share, and get a bank to approve the senior debt

package. The entire package is sorted and ready to be imple-
mented. The lawyers and accountants are all working away and
have invested huge amounts of time in the expectation that the
deal will complete. The management team have neither the time
nor the resources to run more than one VC down to the wire
so they commit to you.

Then your own Investment Committee rejects the deal.

Plaster Wig comes on a visit to Nottingham office and we
complain that 3i is getting a terrible reputation for rejecting and
re-negotiating deals at the last minute. Word is getting around
and there is an increasing risk that we just won't get shown any
more deals. More to the point, there's nothing more personally
excruciating than having to tell a management team who've
placed their trust in you that you can't deliver on the deal you've
agreed with them. What makes it even worse is that controllers
aren't allowed to attend or even listen to the deliberations of
Investment Committee, so we have no chance to defend our case,
query the nature of the objections or just impress on Committee
members the implications of their arbitrary judgements. Plaster
Wig makes soothing noises, but it's essentially clear he doesn't
care. He doesn't have to deal personally with the fallout from
enraged management teams and furious advisers, and there
are so many deals going through that he's not bothered if we
lose a few. He thinks we're just barking at the moon when we
claim that we're losing opportunities because people no longer
trust us. His view is that we are ungrateful sods; we should be
thankful for Investment Committee sharing their many years
of investment experience and great commercial wisdom with us.

This is exactly what happens when we put Nottingham
Group to Investment Committee. The minute says not approved
because the deal is 'too good for management'. How patronising

is that? It's like having to tell your girlfriend you can't see her anymore because your mum thinks she's not good enough for you.

Anyway, is there really a problem with the terms of the deal? Or is this just Investment Committee finding an excuse not to do the deal because it's just too frighteningly big for them? Dogfight is not taking any shit from them and insists we have another go. I have to renegotiate the equity percentage though and the fact that David is so calm, civil and utterly reasonable about the whole thing makes me feel even shittier. The truth is, it's too late for the management to go elsewhere. When I resubmit the deal to Committee with the revised terms, Flagpole calls me to tell me it's now been approved.

'Seems Committee was right about the terms,' he remarks smugly. Silently, I contemplate murder.

Completion meetings are a circus and something of a rite of passage.

There are so many parties involved in getting a large deal done, particularly when we're buying two companies at the same time and each deal comes with more hangers-on than the King of Persia, so the only way to get them all to agree is to get them into one building and not let them leave until everything is signed. And there is a lot to sign: the finalised pack of agreements and appendices and codicils runs to at least a thousand pages and is actually referred to as a 'bible'. I can see why – it's vast, impenetrable, largely make-believe, and once deposited in the drawer no one ever gets it out again to read it.

I can finally see why we're called 'controllers': directing this circus and keeping the momentum up is like conducting an orchestra where each section is playing a different piece of music. In different rooms.

The completion meeting takes three days. Towards the end of the first day I send one of our junior lawyers – a rather dashing young man – off with the lawyer for the mezzanine lender – an attractive young lady of similar age – to a separate room to negotiate and finalise the mezzanine loan and inter-creditor agreements. Two days later it's approaching midnight – which I have set as a deadline for getting the deal over the line – when I suddenly remember the mezzanine documentation. While the main documents are being finalised in the boardroom I set off to track down the two mezzanine lawyers, which involves wandering through empty and echoing corridors, opening closed doors and poking my nose inside. Eventually I detect a noise that sounds remarkably like giggling and follow it to a closed door which, when opened, reveals the two lawyers sitting at a table, a pile of documents off to one side while in front of them are two empty wine bottles and a pile of takeaway pizza boxes. Whilst not exactly undressed, let's say their clothing indicates a certain lack of formality. When I enter the room, the giggling stops and the two of them look startled and deeply guilty. I feel annoyed but, at the same time, rather envious. I would very much have preferred to have spent the last 48 hours drinking and flirting. I ask them if they've sorted out the mezzanine documentation and they exchange a slightly haunted look. I don't know exactly what they've been doing for two days but I'm pretty sure it had little to do with Clause 4 Paragraph (d) subsection (i)(g) defining the standstill provisions in the event of default.

'With you in half an hour,' says my lawyer.

Within thirty minutes the pair of them are back in the boardroom, smartly dressed and looking entirely professional, with their documents fully sorted and ready for signature.

I think the lesson is to start each completion meeting with

a three-day party with wine and pizza and then deal with the legal stuff in the last half hour before going home.

The completion takes place in London and I don't get to bed until after 2 a.m. The reality of what I have just done doesn't hit me until I wake up the next morning. Nobody at 3i has ever led a deal like this before. I make my way slowly back to the office where I am treated like a conquering hero.

Fingers crossed that this one makes money. If it doesn't, I really am going to have to find a new career.

The total equity investment in Nottingham Group is about £14m but I'm told we have to syndicate this on the basis that we can't hold more than a minority stake and couldn't afford to lose £14m in one deal. What? Our balance sheet is only £3.5bn! It's not as though a £14m-sized meteorite crashing into a £3.5bn-sized planet is going to represent an extinction event, is it?

But it's a direct order, so, having fought off any number of other competitors for the deal, I am now instructed by my bosses to give them back what I just stole off their plates. I'm told to sell down our investment to £2m, which means giving no fewer than six other private equity firms an investment without them so much as lifting a finger to earn it. It's like winning an Olympic gold medal and then being told to saw it into seven equal pieces and hand six of them around to the other competitors.

Even more frustratingly, if you have to do this mad thing, there's a crazy logic that the best firms to syndicate to are those that competed directly with you for the deal, on the basis that they already know the business and have their approvals in place. What's even more absurd is that, whatever silky smooth explanation you gave to your own Investment Committee, you probably only won the deal by offering better terms than the competition. But because your competitors have invested so much time and money in the deal, it actually makes sense for them to do it on terms they previously rejected just so the whole project doesn't become a waste of time and money. So now you all get to do the deal on the least attractive terms – it's a race to the bottom.

There's also a lot of peacocking involved. Graciousness and dignity in defeat are qualities not much in evidence in the private equity community. On hearing that he's going to be rewarded with a slice of the deal, the investment executive from CVC, who is ex-3i and lost the beauty parade, gleefully calls me up to gloat, pointing out how much his bonus and investment carry is going to be worth.[22] He knows that 3i doesn't give out carry or pay bonuses, so I won't make anything personally from the deal.

Nevertheless, one unexpected side effect of the deal is that I suddenly become a target for recruitment by other firms. I'm invited out for a beer by another former controller who has joined one of our competitors, who wants me to come for an interview with his firm. It is a dispiriting and annoying encounter. He spends half the time going on about how much his carry scheme is worth and the other half slagging off 3i.

'You know what says it all about 3i?' he enquires, although I don't think he's actually soliciting my opinion. 'The fact that

---

22 Carry is where the investment executive is personally given a share of the deal profits. There's a more detailed explanation of carry in the final chapter: *The Ladder and the Snake.*

you refer to management as "customers". Management aren't customers – it's the other way around! *We're* the customer. The whole process whereby we allow management teams to choose their investors is wrong. It's not management buying the company, it's the investor and it's *their* job to deliver on *our* investment objectives.'

He has a point, of course. But he's also missing the point. Thinking of management as customers is what helps us win deals by creating strong relationships with management teams who, let's face it, are the ones really doing all the work. All we do is manipulate the financial structures and hand out large dollops of cash (ahem, I mean *'deploy our distinct blend of financial and industrial skills to help businesses grow'*). I understand where he's coming from though: it's that old seductive tug about reversing the roles of butler and master of the house. But, the more I learn, the clearer it becomes how little we know. If you stop thinking of management teams as customers, it's a short step to thinking you're really the owner of the business and you know better. That would be fine if we did know better but we're a bunch of ridiculously young, middle-class, grammar school boys and girls and we know fuck all about anything. Having a big cheque book is the financial equivalent of celebrity though; it's all too easy to mistake attention for talent.

The prospect of moving to the competition *is* tempting though: significantly better pay, the freedom to focus on large MBOs and the riddance of the many frustrations of working in clunky, ponderous, ridiculously conservative 3i. Unfortunately, his manner is so arrogant and offensive that it triggers me into a vigorous defence of my company. It's like when someone insults you and you know it's immature and pathetic but you just can't stop yourself from insulting them right back. Anyway, after this I can't exactly accept his job offer. Looks like I'll be staying a bit longer.

Non-executive chairmen are 'a good thing' and every company should have one. This is the party line.

3i has the right to appoint a non-executive chairman to the Board of Nottingham Group, and the process of finding and selecting one is professionally set up and handled by David who, after wide consultation with the investors, comes up with a shortlist of three candidates. We set aside a couple of days to interview them, and come up with an agreed list of questions and issues for discussion. David has selected the candidates to provide a degree of diversity: there is the ex-CEO of a mail order business (sector experience), a professional chairman (chairman experience) and, intriguingly, a candidate with a reputation as a hands-on turnaround specialist.

The sector specialist, as it turns out, doesn't know much about the sector. The professional chairman is urbane and speaks knowledgeably about corporate governance, the role of audit and remuneration committees, organisational development and stakeholder management. At the end of the two-hour interview I realise I stopped listening one hour and fifty-five minutes ago.

The final candidate is the company doctor who, rather in character, turns out to be a gruff, taciturn Yorkshireman who never quite settles into the interview and gives mostly surly, monosyllabic answers. One of the pre-prepared questions seeks his views on remuneration policy and, in particular, the role and extent of directors' bonus schemes.

He looks like he's just been told to put on a wellington boot filled with dogshit. For a moment he tries to frame a diplomatic response. He fails.

'Well, I have a bloody simple approach to remuneration,' he says in his bluff, Yorkshire, nothing-to-see-here accent. 'If someone does a bloody good job, then I bloody well let them keep it.'

Unsurprisingly, David and the team vote for the professional chairman on the basis that he clearly understands what the deal is with these appointments. Don't interfere or make your presence felt and we won't complain about your salary or options package. I'm happy to go along with that. For an easy life.

June 1990 to November 1991

It is expected that I participate in an interminable round of lunches, dinners and corporate hospitality events with lawyers and accountants. This is one of those quirky conventions of commercial life that require you to invest in additional social interaction with people you already spend so much of your working life with that the *last* thing you want to do is spend social time with them as well. The absolute worst are the black-tie dinners: the CBI, the Institute of Directors, the Nottingham Chamber of Commerce, the Society of Lace Manufacturers, the Institute of Chartered Accountants, the Society for Putting Things on Top of Other Things. For these ceremonial events you get into your dinner jacket – probably still bearing mysterious stains from an identical dinner the night before – fish out the synthetic bow tie with the clasp at the back, and locate (after much rummaging) your cufflinks, which for some reason you stuffed in a different pocket. In a small gesture of juvenile defiance, the pair of cufflinks I prefer for these events consists of a 'willie hand' and a 'cheerful penis'. With your shoes freshly shined, you assemble in some cavernous banking hall or hotel anteroom for drinks and small talk. And circulate. Some people are excellent circulators and can greet you like a long-lost brother, exchange a banality and then graciously dump you for the next group in less than a minute. Like the majority, I am a very poor circulator and become skilled at scanning a room of identically-dressed men in black suits and white shirts – like a flock of walking, talking pints of Guinness[23]– for a safe group of people I actually recognise, and rapidly integrate with them. Inevitably we end up looking like a knot of sulky oysters clumping forlornly to a rock after the sea has drained away, pecked at by the aggressive beaks of circulating seagulls. Obesity and boredom are your constant companions in this cycle of forced conviviality. You eat too much and you drink too much because you're bored and because it dulls the edge.

Today I'm having lunch with the senior partner at a prominent legal firm in Nottingham. He is a genial soul, well into his fifties, who hasn't looked at a legal agreement in twenty years. His main role now is to lunch and dine prospective clients and, given my rising prominence in the local business community, he has me scheduled in for lunch at one of Nottingham's finest restaurants at least once a month. The years of dining out on a corporate account have accumulated around his torso and on his face, where his skin resembles a sheet of taut, moist, putty into which his features have been softly pressed from the reverse side. His chin hangs down under his jaw like a stork's gullet. I shouldn't really complain because, as these things go, he's actually relatively easy company. But, all the same, he only has one conversation, which involves remarking on the marvellous

---

23 What *is* the collective noun for an assembly of pints of Guinness? I use 'flock' here because I'm thinking of penguins.

way in which everyone in the Nottingham professional and corporate community is doing so terribly, terribly well. It's the same chat he has been having every lunch and every dinner for twenty years, except he inserts the name of his guest and their firm in at the relevant sections, like a word processor on 'find and replace'. Is this what twenty years of sticky toffee pudding is going to do to me? But the alternative – getting through the lunch without a drink or without the comfort of the rather excellent food on offer – is just too horrible to contemplate.

Fortunately, though, this morning – 2nd August 1990 – my radio woke me up with the news that Iraq has invaded Kuwait. Like most people, I doubt I could find Kuwait on the map. This is serious though: the economic repercussions could be catastrophic and people are losing not just their livelihoods but their lives, too. The world is going to war.

I say 'fortunately' because at least it gives us something to talk about.

Nottingham Group produces its first set of management accounts since the MBO completed. They're not only ahead of budget but *well* ahead.

It's relief rather than euphoria. I've had enough of losing money. I wish I could say it marked some kind of progression in my commercial insight but it doesn't feel that way at all. I liked the company and admired the management team in a way I never did with my previous investments, but that still seems like a terribly flimsy and subjective way to distinguish a good investment from a bad one. The truth is that I'm not sure I'm doing anything fundamentally different; it's just a change in the wind.

3i MEMORANDUM

From: **Paul Traynor**
To: File
Date: 24th October 1990
Subject: Denby Pottery

Following an introduction from BDO Stoy Hayward, Bernard and I visited Denby, which operates out of a huge, rambling old building based in Denby, Derbyshire. The company was actually founded in 1804 and moved to its present site in 1834 in order to take advantage of the nearby clay pit (now long extinguished). The company was acquired by Coloroll Group – the acquisitive conglomerate – in 1987, who introduced the present management team led by CEO Stephen Riley.

Coloroll has now failed and the administrator is selling off all the assets, of which Denby is one of the smaller ones. 1989 operating profit was c.£900k on sales of £10m. Because of the publicity surrounding Coloroll, it's basically now open season on all the subsidiaries and Denby management report that they believe the administrator has received over 60 expressions of interest in Denby alone to date. Indicative offers to be submitted within two weeks.

We were given a tour of the factory by Richard Booth, production director. There are obviously issues around production efficiency created by the nature of the building, which dates from a previous era, but within those constraints our impression was that the manufacturing operation is well-organised. There is an extensive product range and considerable investment has been made in marketing in recent years, particularly in the development of particular market segments such as wedding gifts. Management have not yet had the opportunity to prepare a full business plan but they have prepared forecasts that show they are aiming to grow profits to £1.75m within 3 years.

We were extremely impressed by the management team, particularly CEO Stephen Riley, who gave a clear, cogent account of how he expects to achieve the demanding business goals. His background is FMCG marketing and much of the recent marketing efforts seem to be to his personal credit. There is a small executive team who seem experienced and competent and appear to work well together.

Management are keen to submit an indicative offer and are meeting at least six other VCs. A preliminary analysis of the cashflows suggest we could support them for a bid up to c.£6m, assuming £4m of debt.

The next step is to prepare a proposal for them and, in anticipation of a tight timetable, arrange a visit from an industrial adviser. Given the speed with which the transaction is likely to happen, it will be important for us to be prepared to underwrite the whole transaction, including the senior debt. Our ability to do this will be a major advantage for us in competing for the deal.

There is, among venture capitalists and private equity executives, a standard model for handling a first encounter with a management team.

- A few minutes of social chit-chat.
- Give a five-minute pitch on yourself and your firm.
- Quiz the bastards furiously on the business to make sure you do actually want to invest in it.
- Get the fuck out of there without having promised anything.

This is the 'buying' phase and, from the investment executives' point of view, the key is to get through the buying phase having accumulated as much information as possible whilst giving away the absolute minimum about what you are thinking. You might, after all, change your mind once you've had a chance to ponder. Also, if you have already decided it's not a deal you want to do, it avoids the need to say so in the meeting with all the social awkwardness that entails, particularly if they're rude enough to insist on a reason why. You might also find that your Local Director is much less impressed than you are with the company and its prospects. There is no worse sin in the world of venture capital or private equity than to be caught making a commitment that you subsequently have to row back from.

After a few days of reflection you can get off the fence by calling the CEO and either declining to continue (remembering the first rule of bouncing, which is never to set them a hurdle to clear) or telling him you want to go to the next stage. The next stage is:

- Send them very detailed heads of terms littered with caveats, because you still might want to change your mind later or, more likely, somebody in your organisation will change it for you. If this happens it is absolutely essential to be able to draw their attention to a clause in the heads of terms that *exactly* foreshadowed the reason for your change of position.

- Negotiate. Usually the most effective form of negotiation is to just capitulate and give them what they want.
- Get them to agree to 'exclusivity', which means they agree to drop your competitors and work solely with you to complete the deal.

This is the 'selling' phase.

I have, however, worked out that if you want to win deals it's actually better to do it the other way around. That is to say, start with the selling, make a commitment early and let the buying happen down the line. The key is to build a strong rapport with the management team from the first meeting. Under no circumstances mention all the things that could go wrong; they'll be worrying about enough stuff all on their own without you building up their anxieties further. It's a bit risky, though, as things almost certainly *will* go wrong.

Best not to think about that though – instead, bury all their apprehensions. Be upbeat, positive and get right into their Cloud of Stuff.[24]

As professionals, we are taught to soothe, control and organise. Emotion, we are instructed, gets in the way and compromises rationality. But, for a management team, an MBO is an emotional thing: it's exciting but scary, intriguing and

---

24 Credit for describing and naming the Cloud of Stuff goes to my ex-3i colleague and current training partner, Alice Chapman. We arrived at similar methodologies by different routes but Alice is the one who articulated it, refined it and gave it a name.

fascinating, and intimidating too. The stakes are so high that it can be an emotional rollercoaster: one minute you're elated at the prospect of becoming an independent owner of your own business, the next you're plunged into despair when it seems the company will be sold to a trade rival and you'll be fired the next day. The rhythms and routines of your working day will be pulled to pieces as you find yourself dealing with an ever-expanding cohort of suited advisers, bankers and chino-clad consultants, all of whom assault your competence and knowledge by firing salvo after salvo of intrusive, aggressive and often idiotic questions at you. It's like a tornado passing through your life, sucking all your familiar belongings up into the air and spinning them around your head while you frantically try to grab them and put them back where they belong. In the epicentre of this maelstrom, you feel that everybody has an agenda and you don't know who to trust.

When, as a prospective lead investor, you first meet a management team, they might act cool and in control but all of this stuff – and a lot more – will be going round in their heads and in their guts. Can I do this? What happens if we don't pull it off? What is this smartly-dressed person in front of me really thinking and can I trust him or her? What impact is this going to have on my spouse and children? How rich am I going to be? Which members of my team do I want to take with me and are there some who I wouldn't want around if the MBO goes ahead? How much am I going to have to invest personally and how am I going to persuade my partner to re-mortgage the house? This is the Cloud of Stuff – a chaotic bubble of interrelated issues, questions, hopes, fears, problems and opportunities.

The last thing the management team want is to encounter an inscrutable venture capitalist whose only interest is to probe them on their business plan and then leave with a po-face and not a hint of what they're thinking. The way to differentiate yourself is to get into their Cloud of Stuff. Expect it to be emotional and chaotic, and don't think you're going to soothe, control and organise. Try just being a human being; show them that you get it and maybe, since you've seen all this before, you can help them through it. And don't add to their worries by sharing a load of yours, like whether you'll be able to persuade an industrial adviser to come out within three months or whether there's any prospect of Investment Committee backing you up on this one. That's *your* Cloud of Stuff, not theirs. But most VC and private equity executives treat the Cloud of Stuff as a minefield of awkwardness to be tiptoed around and, as result, come over as bland, boring clones, unperceptive and devoid of empathy.[25]

By the time we get to the Denby team, they are already fed up with showing people around. There have had dozens of VCs and trade buyers traipsing around and all of them took the factory tour, listened to the management presentation, asked questions about the business and left without giving anything away. The Cloud of Stuff buzzing around their heads is particularly intense, which is not surprising given the violent way their world has just been turned upside down. I'm careful to play back each issue that emerges, whether it's to do with the business or the personal impact of the current situation on them, to make sure I've heard right and to demonstrate that I'm really listening. As happens when you summarise, one issue leads to them disclosing another, and summarising that dislodges another in turn. It's unstructured, chaotic,

---

25 This is me now, speaking in 2020: things don't change. I recently encountered a CEO who had been interviewed by seven different private equity teams as part of a beauty parade process and the only distinguishing characteristic he could recall was that one team weren't wearing ties.

powerful. By the time we're forty minutes into the meeting I sense
we've earned their trust and earned the right to put our issues onto
the table: now is the time for some soothing, control and organisation. I tell them I am absolutely certain that we can help them,
that they seem like a brilliant team and that, for all the challenges,
there is a fantastic opportunity here. It seems to me that their most
critical problem is the speed with which events are unfolding and
the high level of interest being shown in the business. I point out
that 3i has the experience and financial capacity to move fast and
underwrite the whole deal, eliminating the risk of introducing too
many parties into the transaction. I suggest we put together an
outline proposal for them on valuation and management equity
and, if they are happy with that, the next step would be for them
to take us through their business plan in detail.

By the time we leave the meeting I sense the deal is ours to
lose. Bernard, though, is horrified. 'We didn't even go through the
business plan and you've told them we'll not only do the deal but
underwrite the whole financing package. You didn't even mention
Investment Committee! Or the industrial adviser!'

'Yep. Scary, isn't it?'

'What are you going to do if Committee bounces it?'

'I'll probably try grovelling. It's worked before.'

Bernard isn't convinced. But Stephen calls me the next day to
say we are their preferred investor and to suggest we come over as
soon as practical to go through the business plan.

I told you it was risky.

Flagpole is away and the Submission for Denby is picked up
by Lickspit, a particularly duplicitous regional director who advises
me that the deal is 'overpriced'. Oddly, though, he is prepared to

allow it to go forward to Investment Committee, but he'll not be recommending it, merely explaining to Committee that they ought to see it. What?

Imperceptibly, my ability to distinguish what is good – or bad – about a business has grown. Despite my misgivings, the period on the portfolio – spending time with so many different businesses and managers without the pressure of having to evaluate a business plan – proved an excellent business education, and my personal research project in the bowels of the Nottingham office was also illuminating. The key, really, is to look for the obvious. Is the company positioned in a growing market or a declining one? Can its customers easily switch to a competitor? Does it enjoy high margins or does it struggle to command prices that cover its costs? Does it have to reinvest all its profits in heavy machinery or marketing just to maintain sales? Do the management seem organised and competent? I think I finally understand why you might not want to invest in a foundry 'in the current climate': foundries are exposed to a lot of competition and have very high fixed costs, meaning they can move very quickly from making profits to making losses if, for example, prices fall in a recession. On the other hand, if sales start to rise, profits accelerate very quickly once the overheads are covered. It's called operational gearing and companies that are highly operationally geared are good ones to invest in on a counter-cyclical basis. In other words, buy in a recession, and sell at the peak. It's like Napoleon said: buy on the sounds of cannons firing.

What confounds this growing sense of commercial confidence is the damnable question of company valuation. It feels good to be developing a more sophisticated evaluation of the strengths and weaknesses of a business but I'm not doing anything that an equally experienced investment executive, or even an informed amateur, couldn't do. The question isn't how good, or weak, a business is

– that's the easy part. The question is how much is it worth? You don't make money by investing in good businesses, you make money by investing in under-priced ones. You can even make money from a weak business if you buy it cheaply enough and it doesn't go bust before you can sell it! What the correct price is for a business doesn't seem to lend itself to the same objective analysis as whether the business is a good one or a bad one.

If someone offers me shares in a foundry on a price-earnings multiple of six, is that cheap or expensive? I know the average stock market multiple is much, much higher than that but then foundries are slow-growth businesses, vulnerable to recession, and this is not a quoted company so I can't bail out of my holding quickly if the share price starts to go south. Is all that fully reflected in a PE ratio of six or not? And it's very hard to resist inferring something about the company from the price it's offered at, which surely has to be the wrong way around. If somebody were to offer me shares in an oil exploration company priced on a PE ratio of two, I wouldn't automatically jump at the bargain; I'd just immediately assume that I am the only person in the world who doesn't know the world just ran out of oil.

All my colleagues seem to have a fluency and assuredness about their arguments on valuation. This comes to a point with Investment Committee, who love to declare that this deal or that deal is 'overpriced' or that the 'terms are too good for management'. There's never an explanation, just a sweeping assertion as though it's *obvious*. But it's never obvious to me. I can't tell just by looking at a company whether it's overpriced, under-priced or fairly priced. All I can do is what I do with Denby, which is to plug the management forecasts into the financial model and keep upping the price until the cashflow turns negative. That's the maximum price you can pay. There's then a debate about the extent to which you can trust the forecasts but, whilst everyone else seems to have their own forceful opinion on this, I can never tell. As David Mansfield said, forecasts are just forecasts. This 'commercial judgement' thing is still proving maddeningly elusive.

Unsurprisingly, given Lickspit's recommendation, the Denby deal is treated harshly by Investment Committee, which rejects it with a crushing verdict of 'no appetite for the business'. Lickspit calls and gleefully skewers me with the news, magnanimously adding a comprehensive personal critique of my commercial analysis and negotiating tactics. He goes on to insinuate that, had I approached him earlier for his assistance, he would have been able to help me avoid this very visible humiliation. Finally the penny drops and I see what's going on here: it's the organisational equivalent of a protection racket. If I want to get these deals approved, I have to go through him and pay him off by allowing him to take credit for the deal.

I am very much not looking forward to making this call to Stephen and the management team. They've not had the time to work with another VC so all their eggs are in our basket and I'm about to tell them that Investment Committee has just thrust a size twelve, hobnail boot right into that basket and pulverised every single egg in it. The chances are now that the team will lose their once-in-a-lifetime opportunity to do an MBO and the business will go to the trade. This is exactly why controllers are so reluctant to give a commitment to a management team. There's clearly something very badly wrong with this process.

I'm about to pick up the telephone to make the dreaded call when it rings. It's our internal property surveyor, who has just returned from a visit to the factory. In all the drama I had actually forgotten that I'd asked him to go. Because I'm proposing to underwrite the senior debt I had thought it a good idea to get the property valued. To be honest, I'm only half-listening as he gives me his views, my mind distracted by the unpleasant conversation I'm going to have as soon as this one finishes. Then I jerk upright.

Say that again.

He's valuing the property at £2m.

Hold on: this is a 200-year-old Victorian building next to an exhausted clay pit in a remote part of Derbyshire. Never mind what it's worth; who on earth would want to buy it in the first place?

I wasn't mishearing things; his valuation is £2m.

I'm caught between curiosity over how on earth he has arrived at this absurd conclusion, and the fear that encouraging him to explain might bring him to his senses. But as I listen to his reasoning it dawns on me that he is, incredibly for someone of his experience, confusing the value of the *property* with the value of the *business*. Clearly, he concedes, nobody in their right mind – or even not in their right mind – would pay anything at all for the building itself or even the land on which it stands, being effectively right next to an exhausted clay pit. But he also reasons that the property must have value to the business that occupies it, if on no other basis than, if the business was forced to relocate elsewhere, it would have to rent alternative premises of a similar size. He has therefore imputed the rent the company might be expected to pay and capitalised this to arrive at his valuation of £2m.

Good God! It is a blatant and horrendous example of circular thinking and I wonder if he's smoking something or displaying the signs of early-onset dementia. But I'm not one to look a gift horse in the mouth so I don't push it beyond making sure he's putting his valuation in writing (I suggest he doesn't need to go into too much detail regarding his workings) in a memo to be forwarded to me as a matter of urgency.

This piece of commercial escapology enables me to immediately resubmit the deal to Committee pointing out that, even if you think £6m is too much to pay for the *company*, it seems that now we are getting a property worth £2m *as well*. This nonsense instantly prompts IC to rediscover their previously non-existent appetite and they approve the deal without a murmur of complaint. It also helps that Flagpole has now returned to the office so I can redirect the revised Submission via him and keep it well away from the Machiavellian interventions of the evil Lickspit.

I feel like a pedestrian who's narrowly avoided being taken out by a rogue driver running a red light at high speed. The deal completes and, as far as I know, Stephen and the management team never know how close they came to losing it.

Three years later Denby floats on the London Stock Exchange and the value soars to £120m. Our £2m equity investment is worth £50m.

£50m is a significant profit for 3i, even if our overall worth is £3.5bn. Yet the investment decision was arrived at with the casualness of someone throwing a torn biscuit wrapper in a roadside rubbish bin, then digging it back out again in case some crumbs had been overlooked. If that's what 'commercial judgement' looks like, then it seems to me we'd be better off without it.

Despite some operational difficulties merging the Arnold operation into the Nottingham warehouse, Nottingham Group is trading well. Denby is also running into some market headwinds but is still managing to improve its trading performance. When we value our investments at the year end, the equity we hold in both companies is judged to have more than doubled in value. Suddenly, making money seems to be just as easy as losing it. Maybe I am gifted at this after all. Or maybe I've just finally found my Thursday ...

It sets me up with an interesting problem, though, because everyone now thinks I have discovered the gift of second sight and become a great investor. Overnight, my lemons are forgotten or dismissed to the training budget. To begin with I try to downplay my new reputation but it's just read as false humility.

Fuck it, if they want to give me the emperor's mantle, I might as well wear it!

3i suffers from the corporate equivalent of FOMA: Fear of Missing Out. We absolutely hate the idea that someone else has done a deal that we would have liked to do ourselves. Corporate FOMA is an addiction that can lead to some strange and unhealthy behaviours. For example, if there's a company up for sale and there are three or four bids for it, it just seems terribly wasteful not to be involved in all of them. That way you're guaranteed not to miss out. Of course, people unfamiliar with the situation might regard this as absurd, disloyal or even potentially illegal. This is where the game of Chinese Walls comes in.

In this game, three separate 3i offices get to look at the same deal. One of them is backing the management team, one is backing an existing portfolio company that wants to make a bid for the company and the third is working with an MBI candidate.

MBI stands for management buy-in and refers to a situation where an experienced but currently unemployed CEO wants us to buy him a job by acquiring the company, kicking out the present CEO and installing him in his place. Think of William the Conqueror eyeing up England and musing that he would make so much better a king than Harold. Naturally, some initial resentment might be expected from the locals but an appropriate flourishing of swords and they'll soon learn to love and appreciate the new ruler. For a time, MBIs are considered a very exciting way to expand the MBO market, until some data shows they are a virtually guaranteed way to lose money. Funny that.

Under the rules of Chinese Walls, no player is allowed to discuss the case with any other player and, indeed, is not supposed to even know the other offices are bidding for the same company. If challenged by our respective 'customers' to explain our apparent involvement in three sides of the same coin, players respond by chiming the words 'Chinese walls', at which point the game moves on to its next phase.

The next phase involves 3i splitting into three equal teams, each of which goes and stands with one of the offices. On each team is an industrial adviser and a regional director. Investment Committee also splits three ways. If any team member attempts to discuss the case with a member of a competing team, they are rebuffed with the words 'Chinese walls'.

Each team is dealt a hand of cards from the pack called *Costs*. A cost card requires you to spend money as specified on the card. For example, a cost card might require you to spend £100k on an accounting report or £75k on legal costs. If the game continues for several rounds, all of the players are likely to accumulate quite a big hand of cost cards.

Players attempt to win the game by making offers to a mysterious figure called The Vendor, whose decision is determined by the spin of a wheel of fortune that declares outcomes such as *Sold to a Competitor* or *Withdrawn from Sale*. The Vendor announces the successful bidder with the phrase *You Have Now Won Exclusivity*, at which point the winning team has their cost cards redeemed by the bank. The losers' cost cards are not redeemed by the bank and they have to quit the game.

To win the game, a player must also draw a card from the Investment Committee pack, which might say *Approved as submitted*, or *You need to renegotiate the terms: go back 3 spaces* or *Committee has No Appetite for the Business: Go back to Square One*. When I get to play Chinese Walls for the first time, all three teams simultaneously draw *No Appetite for the Business* cards and the game ends early.

We suspect that IC realised we were all just bidding against ourselves, which is absurd. They're right of course: it *is* absurd. But how are we supposed to play the game if they're going to peek over the walls?

> I have £75m in cash I need to get rid of in a hurry. Can anyone think of a faster way of disposing of it than tearing up the notes one by one and flushing them down the toilet?
> Answer: Isosceles
> *Humour section of 3i Staff Magazine, Autumn 1991*

The MBO party is heating up. Down in London, firms such as CinVen, CVC, Candover and Electra – largely staffed by investment executives poached from 3i – are proliferating and flourishing, filling their boots on MBOs, which are getting more numerous, larger in size, and more and more profitable. In the world of venture capital, large MBOs are apples in the Garden of Eden, but for some reason 3i doesn't want to take a bite.

3i is like the geeky teenager hanging around the kitchen at the party – it doesn't want to be left out but it lacks the confidence to join in. 3i management is fearful of losing large sums of money and convinced that our competitors are paying reckless prices for deals. But it's hard to stay off the dance floor when everyone else seems to be having so much fun. In 1989, 3i summons up its courage and decides to take a £75m equity participation in the £2.2bn leveraged acquisition of the Gateway supermarket chain. It is fashionable to give the buyout vehicle a snazzy name and the Gateway mega-buyout is branded Isosceles, a name that will become infamous in the UK buyout community. From the outset the deal is a disaster, the company completely swamped by the mountain of debt. In less than two years, our entire investment is wiped out by a restructuring. Unsurprisingly, the debacle triggers a massive loss of mojo and 3i slinks resentfully back into the kitchen. Investment Committee becomes very wary and clamps down on deals coming through, rejecting lots because they're 'overpriced' or the terms are 'too good for management'. It's like we've sent an expeditionary party out into the jungle and they've come back some time later, depleted, bedraggled and raving about horned monsters. Nobody's going back out there again!

No doubt, a lot of the resistance to large MBOs is a result of the Isosceles horror show but all the other MBOs we do seem to make money and do so quickly. Once the dam is broken with Nottingham Group, it doesn't take long before other controllers in other regional offices start pitching for and winning leads in bigger MBO transactions. The way we win these deals is simply by deploying the qualities traditionally associated with 3i's approach to the smaller company market: working with local advisers, building a rapport with the management team and treating them like customers rather than pawns in a transactional game. Most of all, it's the 3i core value: a ferocious willingness to have a go, to make something happen and take on the innate conservatism of our own organisation. Every venture capital deal, small or large, is born to the clamour of a thousand reasons why it won't work or won't happen, and if you allow yourself to listen to that or show your anxiety to the management team, you'll miss out on the party.

For all its quirks and idiosyncrasies, 3i is a formidable deal-making machine when it gets up a head of steam. Most investors – cautious, sceptical souls – approach each investment with the question, 'why should I do this deal?'

3i controllers start with, 'why not?'

Before I leave Nottingham there is one more deal to do.

The Nottingham audit partner of Arthur Andersen calls me with a story about a client and a problem. His client, Humberside Holdings, is the operator of a number of haulage and distribution facilities at Humberside port. At this time the government is embarking on the privatisation of UK ports and one of the first on the block is the Tees & Hartlepool Port Authority. Humberside Holdings wants to make a bid but the price tag is likely to be around £70m-£80m and they don't have – nor can they expect to borrow – that sort of money. Interestingly, a shareholder in Humberside Holdings is Powell Duffryn, a substantial quoted business. Powell most certainly do have the cash to make a bid for Teesside but think it wouldn't go down well with their shareholders, who would see it as splashing out on something not relevant to the core business. Powell Duffryn is prepared to make a contribution but they can't be seen to take more than 50% of the venture. Actually this suits the shareholders of HH, who want a share of the equity themselves.

The audit partner explains that he's been puzzling over this one. There is an interesting deal in there somewhere, he's sure of it, but it doesn't seem to fall into any obvious category. It isn't a straight acquisition, it isn't a debt deal and it isn't a management buyout. Can we help?

'Why not?' I say.

We put together a consortium bid with 3i, HH and Powell holding a third each. 3i invests £8.5m.

I'm getting very good at writing Submissions. The tone is important: it has to be dispassionate and authoritative, like you've objectively considered every possible angle and arrived at the well-evidenced conclusion that this is a deal that should, on balance, be done. Never gush over a proposition, make sure you identify and articulate a number of risks, and write it as though quietly sharing, with a colleague blessed with as much commercial judgement as you, your belief that this is an attractive opportunity. Always assert that you have faced stiff competition for the deal but have nevertheless succeeded in winning it (even if you haven't yet) on better terms than the competition is offering because management value 3i's long-term, hands-off approach. Describe the CEO as driven, strategic and dynamic but possessing great attention to detail, and the finance director as tough and focused on cost control. Most importantly, you need to state that, while you believe the forecasts to be achievable, you are worldly enough to appreciate that forecasting is an art rather than a science and budgets can always be missed. Accordingly you have modelled a realistic 'downside' scenario showing that, even if the company fails to generate sufficient cash to pay dividends, it could still service its debt and therefore your capital will remain safe even in adverse circumstances.

If you've done a good job, the experience of reading the Submission will be like a warm bath in a candlelit room: comforting, relaxing, soothing and liable to cause you to nod off before the end. For the first time, a deal of mine goes through Investment Committee without complaint and they don't even make me syndicate away our investment. I'm sure it was because my Submission was more mollifying than a packet of Prozac although, disappointingly, I am told some time later by one member of Committee that there was very little discussion about the business prospects or the pricing. Apparently, the day was very swiftly carried when someone declared that nobody ever failed to make money buying things from the government. Cue much nodding of heads and a quick 'Approved as submitted'.

There's a sealed bid auction and somehow – I'm not sure I want to know too much about it – our consortium emerges as the preferred bidder and the deal completes.

The company performs so well that, within two years, Powell Duffryn find themselves in the awkward position that a substantial portion of their group profits are derived from a company over which they have no control. They have no choice but to buy us out. We sell our £1.5m stake for a profit of £60m, having already been repaid the remaining £6m plus a healthy stream of dividends.

When news of the deal breaks, there is a fair degree of press coverage along the lines of the government haplessly giving away public assets on the cheap. The *Sunday Times* runs an article making vague accusations that seem to imply that one of the Humberside Holdings non-executive directors, who wasn't involved in the deal, has been guilty in the past of sailing close to the wind. As a result, I'm summoned to London and given a bollocking for not doing my due diligence properly and bringing 3i into disrepute.

Strikes me as a bit unfair.

8

THE LADDER AND THE SNAKE

'For every snake, there is a ladder; for every
ladder, a snake.'

Salman Rushdie, Midnight's Children

Six years after I had been offered the option to join the London City Office as a trainee and chose Birmingham instead, I end up there anyway as a newly-minted Local Director.

In 1945 the Industrial and Commercial Finance Corporation (ICFC) was founded to provide finance for small and medium-sized firms and in the same year a separate business, the Finance Corporation for Industry (FCI), was established to focus on large companies. In 1973 FCI was acquired by ICFC and renamed Finance for Industry (FFI). ICFC was rebranded Investors in Industry in 1983 and privatised as 3i eleven years later. Whereas the ICFC part of 3i continued to flourish, FFI never really found a meaningful role for itself. But, like a piece of old junk you can't quite bring yourself to throw out against the possibility that you might one day find a use for it, it was retained in the form of a small team based in London and kept separate from the ICFC teams. Somewhere along the way, FFI was renamed 'City Office'.

As the large MBO market started to develop in London through private equity firms like Candover, Electra and CinVen, City Office was awarded something of a cautious watching brief. The Tenth Floor, dominated by ICFC staff whose entire background and training was in small growth capital investing, was by instinct very wary of larger deals, fearing the opportunity to lose a lot of money very quickly. The Isosceles debacle rather vindicated this anxiety. However, you can only hang around so long in the Garden of Eden before that apple starts to look really, really tempting …

In the Autumn of 1991 the Tenth Floor finally breaks and decides to get into the larger MBO market in a serious way. It makes two decisions.

The first is to rename City Office as the Large Companies Unit. Nobody's quite sure how that helps.

The second is to transfer me into the unit to ginger them up a bit.

Being promoted to Local Director is a big thing, the biggest. Every controller wants to make it to LD. When my promotion comes through I am, naturally enough, extremely pleased with myself.

I call my parents to tell them the news. It's not as though I speak to them very much, so that's probably a good indication of how smug I'm feeling.

My mother is not impressed. She counters by drawing my attention to the fact that Duncan Gray, who was my best friend when I was ten, has just been made assistant manager of the new Tesco superstore in Gravesend. And he didn't even go to university. She also takes the opportunity to remind me pointedly – if a bit laterally – that he is married with three children, whereas I remain childless and unmarried.

My father tries to be more positive.

'Very good, Paul. Well done.'

There's an uncomfortable pause while we both wait for further conversation to materialise. It's like waiting for a bus on a route that's been taken out of service years ago.

'Good. Very good,' he finally volunteers. 'So, what *exactly* does a Local Inspector do then?'

I don't exactly warm to 3i London when I arrive. More to the point, 3i London doesn't exactly warm to me. I'm not expecting to be greeted with blaring trumpets and a triumphal procession but I was hoping for something more welcoming than a small, windowless office and a wall of indifference.

It starts with the building. There's no elegant townhouse reminding me of *The Magic Faraway Tree* – just a vertical turd of a modern building in brown glass and steel girders on top of a plate glass atrium. Even the location is classless – Waterloo Road, right opposite the station. Other than the Greek takeaway next door, which looks like a snappy white puppy that's bitten the building's ankle and won't let go, there are no cafés, restaurants or bars nearby apart from a tiny pub around by the Royal Legion where the carpet reeks of stale beer and cigarette smoke, and the Archduke, a vulgar wine bar under the railway arches. Nearby is The Cut, with market stalls and knock-off shops, and in the other direction lie the subterranean honeycomb of passages that reach under the Southbank centre like tangled concrete roots, stinking of piss and through which well-dressed city commuters must run a daily gauntlet of the homeless, shored up against the winter cold with cardboard boxes once occupied by smart Japanese televisions or IBM laptops.

Inside, 3i Head Office is pleasant but synthetic. The building is like a vertical filing cabinet with floors for drawers, each labelled with the contents: Premises Department on the first, a suite of meeting rooms on the fifth, Tax on the sixth, HR on the eighth. The four regional teams are on the fourth floor while the Large Companies Unit is on the second. Management are, of course, on the upper floors (why does altitude always go with seniority? It has to be a God complex, right?), with regional directors on the ninth and ExCo, including the CEO, on the tenth. The only break to the pattern is the staff canteen on the eleventh floor, where a strict, unwritten, apartheid operates: secretaries and support staff take their lunch from 12 to 12:30, controllers and Local Directors from 12:30 to 1:00, and regional and executive directors exclusively after 1 .p.m. Occasionally the CEO decides to mingle and materialises in one of the earlier slots, plonking his food-laden tray down next to some hapless junior controller and initiating conversation. Accordingly, controllers learn to eat fast with one eye on the entrance and, if the CEO puts in an appearance, scatter like penguins spotting an approaching polar bear.

On the investment floors, the directors have private offices around the edge of the building while the controllers and secretaries are strewn across the interior, stashed behind breast-high partitions to create a degree of privacy. It's more like the claims department of an insurance company than a regional 3i office.

Cul-de-Sac is the regional director in charge of the Large Companies Unit. He's a small, fussy man, and if he turned sideways you'd probably lose sight of him, apart from his librarian glasses. He boasts an impeccable investment track record, which has been achieved, as far as I can tell, by the simple means of never investing in anything at all. Nevertheless, his command of investment and market vocabulary is exemplary. Within half an hour I have had my ears boxed with terminology such as 'strip integrity', 'PIK roll-ups', 'execution risk', 'resource management' and 'contingency exposure'. I haven't a clue what he's talking about. Still, he gives me a small team and a complex portfolio case to settle me in: British Printing and Packaging Corporation Limited.

It's all a bit underwhelming, really. Still, chin up! I'm sure things will improve once I get a chance to settle in.

I've never been called by a headhunter before. It's actually rather flattering, not to mention a little bit exciting. It's tricky to find the balance between acting cool whilst showing just the right level of interest.

The headhunter specialises in matching up disaffected 3i controllers, especially those in London, with MBO firms. He's doing a roaring trade.

He's heard that I've recently arrived in London and wants my permission to offer me around the market. Eventually, after I've milked the telephone call for all the attention I can get, I admit that, whilst I appreciate the call and would love to stay in touch, I'm not quite ready to consider a move yet. I want to see how I get on in London first.

He's very nice about it and doesn't try and hard-sell it. He concludes the conversation by asking me if there's anyone else I would suggest he approach. I immediately recommend three controllers who in my opinion are totally incompetent, in the hope that he'll find another job for them.

After I've put the phone down a question occurs to me: where did he get my name from?

It doesn't help that my arrival in London coincides with the UK going into recession.

The Loadsamoney boom of the 1980s overheats the economy and, in an effort to tame inflation, Britain joins the Exchange Rate Mechanism in October 1990. Unfortunately, at pretty much the same time, German interest rates shoot up to fund the costs of reunification and British rates have to follow them. The interest rate hike causes a recession that starts in July 1990 and deepens during 1991.

Professionally speaking, I've never lived through a recession before. It's kind of scary interesting. Falling sales and high interest rates are NOT good for companies carrying a lot of debt, which applies to management buyouts in particular. Also our deal flow drops right off so there's less investing to do, which is just boring. Obviously I retain a deep personal interest in how my previous investments are doing. Having finally gathered a few plums, I am more than a little anxious that they're about to turn into lemons before they've had a chance to ripen.

P K Stationery got refinanced a couple of times and then went bust. Neil continued to be an arse, and the strong chairman hoovered a strong salary out of the company for a while but was otherwise completely ineffective. The business never opened enough shops to achieve critical mass and the shops it did open never achieved anything like the sales expected. The next time I get an industrial adviser's report that says he can't see anything wrong with the business, it's going straight into the Deal Rejected bin.

CMS proceeded straight into the land of the living dead where it presumably continues to drive around, purposefully but pointlessly, like a Vauxhall Cavalier in a TV advert.

The news from Nottingham is mixed, but overall a bit better.

Fitchett continues to struggle. Builders' merchants do not do well in recessions and the company has missed its forecasts by a mile, which means it can't afford to pay the interest on its loans. That doesn't mean it's going to go bust; we've had to put more equity in to fund the interest payments, which hopefully will just mean we make lower returns rather than take a write-off. It's touch and go, though. Whitmore's is still doing well but it's a relatively small company.

Nottingham Group is doing well, despite having encountered some problems integrating the Arnold operations into the Nottingham warehouse. But sales are relatively recession-proof and they're going to beat the forecasts. On the other hand Denby, as a consumer-dependent business, has been hit hard by the economic downturn and the workforce had to be put onto a three-day week. Having said that, Stephen and the team seem to be managing the situation brilliantly and, financially speaking, have even overachieved against their budgets. As for Teesside, the recession has had about as much impact on that monolith of a business as a mild summer breeze on an aircraft carrier at flank speed. Profits and cashflow are racing ahead of forecast and it looks like the company will be repaying its loans early.

When our annual accounts get produced they show massive uplifts in value for Nottingham Group, Denby and Teesside. So overall I am hugely in credit, even allowing for the loss of P K Stationery and Samji, and the underperformance at Fitchett and CMS. The valuations are derived by finding an appropriate price earnings ratio comparison from the stock market. Even after applying a hefty discount for the fact that the business is unquoted, this still makes the companies worth far more than what we paid for them, simply because market PE ratios are so much higher than the ones we use when pricing for an investment. It's a theoretical value though: we won't know for real if we've made money until the companies are sold to a trade buyer or float on the stock market themselves.

It's funny, though. All the satisfaction when a deal goes well is nothing compared to the lingering angst at your failures. Thinking about Samji, P K Stationery and Fitchett stirs up a physical uneasiness in my gut that is never quite soothed by Nottingham Group, Denby or Teesside. The lemons may be outweighed by the plums, but the sour taste of fiasco never fades.

What's also obvious is how my successes are as much down to *what* I've been doing as to *how* I've been doing it. Buyouts are just so much more profitable than growth capital.

That's a trend that is reflected in the industry as a whole. There's a massive swing away from traditional growth capital investing and towards management buyouts, the bigger the better. That's where Thursday is – and all the fun too.

I've been here in London a few weeks now and can't hide it from myself any longer. This is awful.

Becoming a Local Director is supposed to be the moment you've made it. You get independence, your own patch and your own team. You get status in the local business community and you get respect. You even get your own approval authority, which is to say you can approve Submissions (in my case as a junior

LD, up to £125,000). Being a Local Director normally puts you at the top of the pile: you represent 3i in your city and when the deals come in you get to decide which controller works on them. In London, none of this is true. I am just one of at least eight Local Directors, including four in the Large Companies Unit alone. It's true that the London market is teeming with advisers, which also means that it's teeming with deals, but it's also teeming with other LDs and controllers who are just as much competition for deals as the hundreds of outside venture capitalists and buyout firms.

Stepping out of a regional office and into London is like being a small fish poured into the open sea after growing up in a tropical fish tank. Previously, I was the biggest fish in the tank, now I'm just one of thousands milling around on a vast coral reef. Since, in the Large Companies Unit, we only do deals over £10m, I don't even get to use my shiny new approval authority. £125k wouldn't cover the legal fees on a large MBO.

In fact, it's worse than that. When I joined Birmingham and subsequently Nottingham, I was welcomed as an addition to the team. Here, I'm just another new face with a reputation as an effective deal-doer. That doesn't make me a valued colleague: it makes me a threat. Apart from the dreaded cold calling, the only way to get to a deal in the London market is via one of the many advisers. But I don't know any of the London advisers and they certainly don't know me. We have a comprehensive marketing database but my new colleagues make it abundantly clear to me that it would be taken as a declaration of war if I were to contact any adviser whose name did not have my initials against him or her on the database. There *are*, of course, no advisers on the database with my initials against them. To be fair, with the recession biting deals are pretty scarce, so none of the other London LDs are going to volunteer to hand over a precious marketing asset to a newcomer. I'm sure I would be the same. I point this out to Cul-de-Sac but his response is a shrug. He says it's not his job to 'spoon-feed' me. I'm a Local Director now and should just get on my bike and do some marketing.

The truth is that the number of deals coming to the market has dropped by at least half and, fearful for the economic outlook, Investment Committee is being very tough on those at which we do get to pitch. The simple equation is that there are too many investment staff now and not enough deals. We're all left like stranded revellers competing for a taxi at 2 a.m. on New Year's Day.

When I was a kid, I had a Snakes & Ladders board. The biggest snake of all was the one with its mouth on the penultimate square and if you landed on it, you slid all the way down to the start. The move from Nottingham to London was supposed to be the final ladder but it feels instead that I've just landed on that snake's mouth and I'm slithering all the way down its curly spine right back to square one.

BPCC is a deal straight out of *Barbarians at the Gate* or Isosceles. It's a printing and packaging conglomerate staggering around under a vast mountain of debt, like a drunk giving a piggyback to a very fat person. The company is carrying over £350m of finance, most of which was used to buy the company off the bankrupt Robert Maxwell, while the rest is a consequence of BPCC management's subsequent aggressive acquisition spree. It's been a wholesome disaster and now needs refinancing. We have a small position in the £40m mezzanine strip, alongside eleven other mezzanine investors, which is trapped between

£160m of senior debt and £150m of equity. I'm sent along to a meeting to meet the management and discuss the refinancing.

Call me a traditionalist but, to me, a meeting is where you meet people, discuss the matter in hand, and try to agree a mutually beneficial outcome. This is something else entirely. The company has booked a 200-seat conference centre and even then there is standing room only. There must be sixty banks represented, and bankers always travel in threes (together with their advisers). There are also twenty venture capital funds and the twelve mezzanine providers, both also travelling in twos (plus advisers). And then there's me (no advisers).

The management team sit on an elevated stage flanked by accountants, consultants and lawyers and make a presentation on the business plan, which consists of stunningly colourful and impressive graphics conveying absolutely nothing of use or interest at all. This is followed by an equally pyrotechnical presentation from a firm of accountants, who have been hired at great expense to conduct an 'independent' due diligence review, which is equally devoid of content. It is impossible to glean anything from either the presentations or the sterile Q&A session that follows – other than that the CEO is completely up his own arse and accepts absolutely no responsibility for the dire situation in which the company finds itself. Next to me, in a row of seats near to the back of the hall, five Japanese bankers sleep contentedly with their chins on their chests.

Following this snooze fest, I discover that 3i is joint leader of the mezzanine strip and I receive a dozen-page document from the lead equity investor proposing the terms of the refinancing. This is clearly slanted to the advantage of the equity strip and is merely the opening volley of shots in what promises to be an extremely complicated negotiation. Personally, I'd squirt strychnine into the whole nest of vipers, but that's not an option – our consent is required even if we refuse to put more money in. Over the next few days, competing proposals and counter-proposals and counter-counterproposals pour into my email inbox from various members of the equity, mezzanine and debt syndicates. My fellow mezzanine strip leader calls me up to discuss strategy.

'I think we need to minimise execution risk, manage our contingency exposure and maintain strict strip integrity in exchange for a premium yield roll-up, ideally in the form of PIK notes,' I suggest.

He agrees.

'Can I ask you a personal and sexual question?'

The questioner is a short, tubby, follically-challenged controller. He introduces himself as Harold and confides he doesn't really have a personal and sexual enquiry – it's just a standard icebreaker he uses liberally at networking events with admittedly mixed responses. He wants to introduce himself and offer that, if I ever need any support on a deal, he's more than willing to help out.

Actually, I do have a deal. But the only reason I have it is because no one else will touch it with a bargepole. It's been brought in by a tiny corporate finance boutique nobody has ever heard of. With no existing contact at 3i, they had to resort to phoning the switchboard. Since, in desperation for some new business, I'm back to taking telephone GEs again, the business plan has ended up on my desk. The adviser, David Hudson, explains that he's trying to put together the management buyout of a publicly listed company. The stock market listing is the problem, as stock exchange rules make it practically impossible to mount a management buyout. He's already touted it extensively around the market, but no buyout firm wants to take on a public-to-private transaction.

I should just bounce it really. But I hear David out and the commercial story sounds quite interesting. More to the point, I've got bugger all else to do other than field surreal discussions on BPCC. It can't do any harm to meet the management team. I have very low expectations, though. The company is called Continuous Stationery plc. Even the name is dire.

I don't want to waste Harold's time or his goodwill, so I'm straight with him about the chances of success before I ask him if he'd like to come along to the meeting.

He's up for it.

In the novel *Catch-22*, there's a character called Major Major Major Major, who instructs his assistant not to allow visitors into his office until he's jumped out the back window and hidden in a communications trench. This is, as far as I can tell, the role that the Large Companies Unit plays within 3i. We look at a lot of deals but, if there's the slightest possibility of actually doing one, we jump out the window and hide.

There's also a lot of fear around the recession. Cul-de-Sac deems the market to be 'over-ripe' and 'frothy'– if he's not going to actually do any investing, the least he could do is work on his metaphors – and the downturn has just reinforced his view that we shouldn't be doing any new investing. We do, in fact, still receive a reasonable flow of business plans to look at but we always have a closely-argued reason not to pitch for the lead: the forecasts are too ambitious; the valuation is too 'stretching; we'll never raise the debt in the current climate or – my favourite – the chances of winning are too remote to justify the required 'resource'.

It seems we'd much rather be the bridesmaid than the bride, hanging off the real action in the hope of catching the odd bouquet in the form of a bit of mezzanine here, or participation in a senior debt package there. We're the tramp rummaging for scraps in the bins outside the posh restaurants where our competitors are dining.

It's embarrassing. It's also boring. Deal-doers are like sharks; we have to keep swimming in order to breathe. I'd rather be back in Birmingham doing small deals than sitting in splendour here in the ivory tower doing nothing at all.

There are meetings on meetings on meetings regarding BPCC. Nothing ever gets decided.

Eventually some kind of deal falls into place – if you drop enough spaghetti on a plate, eventually it will arrange itself into some kind of pattern – and a mountain of legal documents are prepared. The day before completion, the CEO announces he will be vetoing the deal unless he gets a substantial pay rise and his required personal contribution to the rescue funding is funded by a 'commitment' bonus.

I'd put the whole thing into administration just to teach the fucker a lesson but I'm in a minority of one. His terms are accepted and the refinancing completes.

Three years later, BPCC floats on the London Stock Exchange for almost exactly the same value at which it was originally acquired from Maxwell Corporation. This is hardly a stunning result and, because it's been through two refinancings, the original private equity backers take a large write down on their investments. On the plus side, the CEO makes a very large personal fortune.

For internal 3i use only

3i MEMORANDUM

From: **Paul Traynor**
To: **File**
Date: **23rd March 1992**
Subject: **Continuous Stationery plc**

This deal was introduced by David Hudson of Campbell Lutyens, a small corporate finance boutique not previously known to 3i. Harold G and I visited both of the two operating subsidiaries to meet the management and establish what kind of deal opportunity, if any, exists.

The company is listed on the London Stock Exchange and was formerly the investment vehicle of two ambitious entrepreneurs who intended to build a substantial conglomerate. This initially attracted strong institutional support and twelve months ago the company was valued by the market at over £40m.

However, the acquisition strategy flopped: only three companies were ever bought, and both the entrepreneurs left the group some time ago, leaving a skeleton group board consisting of the MDs of the three trading subsidiaries and a non-executive chairman. The share price has now collapsed and the market value is just £8m. There is very little trading in the shares, which are held by a mix of shareholders – some institutional, and some private individuals. There is, however, a small group of 3-4 institutional shareholders who, between them, hold a significant minority position. We understand that these have indicated to the board a very strong desire to exit from the company.

Despite the collapse of the share price, group trading is positive with expected sales to 31 March 1992 of £16m likely to deliver a profit of c.£1m. The current share price therefore looks very cheap.

We understand that the board has been actively trying to sell the company for at least a year without managing to generate any serious interest. Campbell Lutyens are advising the management of the main trading subsidiary, Prontaprint (the high-street design and printing franchise with over 200 outlets), who are hoping to undertake a management buyout. However the group board is insisting that any bid is made for the plc itself, principally to avoid adverse tax consequences for the shareholders if the company's assets are sold and the proceeds distributed via a company liquidation.

We met Hudson and the two managing directors of the two main trading companies (Prontaprint and Carwin, a business forms supplier). We didn't go into the business plan in detail but management believe there are significant gains to be made both in revenue and profitability if they can extract themselves from the dead hand of the shell plc.

Our initial thought was that we would only be prepared to look at funding the individual buyouts, due to the various difficulties in mounting a bid for a listed company, but on further investigation it would appear that the greater opportunity may well be to make an offer for the plc itself. The current share price reflects the heavy group costs of maintaining a listing and also the potential tax liability in the event of a liquidation: both of these factors would amount to a significant discount for an incoming investor.

Initial impressions of the operating management were reasonable enough but we would definitely want to introduce a new
group CEO or, possibly, executive chairman, and potentially a new
group FD. Our NX chairman resource has already put forward a
shortlist of potential candidates.

Cul-de-Sac is through to my windowless office faster than
a cat whose tail has been dipped in boiling water. He is bran-
dishing the Pink like a revolutionary with a flag on a street
barricade. He seems agitated. His elbow bangs against the filing
cabinet door and he gives it the sort of look you give someone
who rudely barges into you on a train platform.

He is deeply troubled, he splutters, by my interest in this
Continuous Stationery deal.

Am I aware, he enquires with a tartly raised eyebrow, that this
is a *public-to-private* transaction? Do I fully appreciate the risks
and difficulties of acquiring a company from the *public markets*?
The valuation would *de facto* be excessive and the costs inevitably
beyond control. He's sorry, but there is no way he could endorse
the deployment of *valuable executive resource* on such a specula-
tive adventure. At any rate, the business case seems *intolerably*
weak: by my own admission there are serious management
deficiencies and the *strategic integrity* of the group is highly
questionable. He is sure that, upon proper reflection, I will realise
this is one on which we should pass. He is thoughtful enough
to add that, should any mezzanine or senior debt ultimately be
required, that might possibly be attractively priced.

He has a way of sounding like an academic conducting a
peer review of a science paper, but he's been fixing me with a

furious eye the whole way through this conversation. I think maybe he wants me to drop the case.

I disagree, saying that I appreciate the circumstances are challenging but think the potential upside makes it worth pursuing.

He's flummoxed. In his world, arguing back is as thuggish as slapping his cheek with a gauntlet and proposing a dawn meeting on Blackheath with pistols.

We stare at each other for a bit and then he puts his nose in the air, like someone hurriedly vacating a public lavatory after discovering what the previous occupant left in there unflushed. He says, well, upon my head be it but, if he was me, he would proceed with extreme caution.

I'm tempted to ask if there is any situation where he would encourage me to proceed with reckless abandon. But I manage to bite my tongue.

When he's left, I tell our mutual secretary that perhaps it's a good idea to stop putting my file memos in the Pinks.

Upon my head be it? I think that's the posh version of putting my cock on the block. On the plus side, it's reassuring that he considers me to be a valuable executive resource. I have been getting rather the opposite impression.

I have been asked to design and run a course to pass on my experience in winning large MBOs to controllers. I take a group of senior investment executives from the regional offices away to Creaton for a week and it's a riot, both professionally and personally. I get them to roleplay meeting a management team for the first time and watch with interest to see how they handle it. Most of them very much trade on their personal style, which means they are very effective with some management teams but much less so with others. Any level of self-analysis is non-existent, so we set up video cameras so they can watch themselves. We start to build up a picture of what skills can make a controller more effective – *summarising* being the main one – and give them an opportunity to practice in a simulated environment. It also enables us to see how meetings are structured and I am interested to note how they all follow the traditional method of buying first/selling late, so I show them how you can invert the process. Some of them like it and some of them don't but they all think the course is brilliant. In the evenings we get wholesomely drunk and complain grandiosely about 3i.

It's like being back in a regional office again.

Harold likes to pop in and keep me updated with the gossip.

Kelts, who is a controller in one of the London regional teams and who has a reputation as something of a prankster, dealt with a walk-in GE. Apparently the would-be entrepreneur claimed to have a world-changing invention, which he'd brought with him but was only prepared to reveal once he had a guarantee, in the form of a confidentiality agreement, that we wouldn't steal his idea. We're not really supposed to sign confidentiality agreements, at least not without clearance from our legal department, so there was a bit of a disagreement. But, eventually, and driven mainly out of curiosity to see what the inventor had brought with him, Kelts agreed and signed something. At which point the inventor reached into his bag and produced a cardboard shoebox.

Kelts couldn't help himself. 'It's been done, mate.'

'What?' said the inventor, confused.

'The cardboard box. It's already been done.'

Kelts thought he was being funny but the inventor didn't see it that way. Irreverence is not one of the qualities he is looking for in a venture capital backer, so he stuffed the box back in his bag and walked out in a huff.

The story has gone around the building and we're all mad with Kelts. We want to know what was in the box.

The headhunter is back on the phone. He understands my position but he's been retained by a particular private equity firm to recruit a new partner and he thinks I'd be perfect for the role. How about just meeting for a chat?

The frustrations of working in 3i London aren't going away. I'm still reluctant to quit but I'm feeling a lot less confident than I was that things will turn around.

'Why not?' I reply.

I have a meeting with the managing partner of the VC with whom he's put me in touch. It's a perfectly pleasant encounter but, if I'm honest, a bit serious and mechanical. He is very keen to stress how I will enjoy the more professional approach at his firm, by which I think he means they write much longer investment papers, pay out ten times as much in due diligence fees and attend meetings in threes.

Thoughtfully, he has arranged for one of his team to take me out for lunch so I can ask the sort of questions that he's sure I have but wouldn't want to put to him directly. My potential future colleague takes me to an exquisite restaurant so quiet you can eavesdrop on the conversation five tables away. The food barely covers the plate, the potatoes are Lyonnaise and there is creamed spinach available on the side. My host sticks to fizzy mineral water but is solicitous enough to check whether

I prefer still.

It's not the Shakespeare under New Street Station and everyone in the restaurant is wearing a suit. We talk about the state of the MBO market, and exchange views on pricing and the availability of bank debt. He's very respectful about his boss.

I order a pint of lager just to wind him up and as a private homage to a similar, yet so different, encounter many years ago. I suspect the waiter has to go to the pub next door to get it. Nevertheless, I'm as sober at the end of the meal as I was at the start.

There are many good reasons for jumping ship: the money elsewhere, less internal competition, a more enthusiastic approach to investing than 3i London's suffocating negativity. But I'm just not feeling it. I think it's a question of stubbornness and pride: I don't want to be seen to have made a mistake or failed. People will say that it was easy in Nottingham, where there was no competition, but I couldn't cut it when I got to the London market. I need to prove myself in London first; then I can leave.

I arrange a further set of meetings with the management of Continuous Stationery, accompanied by Harold. I'm beginning to get that feeling of deal desperation again. I know it's dangerous, but I can't help myself. I need to get a deal done. If there's a way to make this work, I'm going to find it.

Ed Carwin is a genial giant of a man who does pretty much all of his business on the golf course. He founded the company, ran it for a number of years and then sold it to Continuous Stationery. Unfortunately, and a little naively, he took shares in the plc as payment. When CS fell out of favour with the market, his shares lost two-thirds of their value and, despite the listing, there were no buyers anyway. Basically, he had ended up selling his company for nothing. Ed wasn't into self-pity, though, so he just dialled down his work ethic and spent more time at the golf club. The company still makes a small profit but is not being driven in any way.

Prontaprint is run by Derek Mottershead, who has a background in marketing. I can't make up my mind about him on first meeting. He says all the right things but somehow doesn't quite convince. Nevertheless, there is a clear opportunity to grow the Prontaprint brand through additional outlets, provided the resources are made available. It is equally clear that both businesses have been neglected within the plc, and I suspect there are all sorts of little things that can be done to improve profits and cashflow by a determined and committed team.

Harold and I also meet a number of potential chairmen, from which one candidate stands out. Richard Raworth is experienced, available, interested and genuinely terrifying.[26]

With a core team in play and a broad understanding of where the commercial upside is, the question becomes how to pull off a deal. I have never done a public-to-private before, so I take myself off to Campbell Lutyens office and get them to talk me through the issues.

When you make an approach for a listed company, the bid is subject to stock exchange regulations, which are essentially designed to wring out the best of terms for the current shareholders. This primarily involves denying the bidder any tactics other than to plonk a fully-funded, public offer down on the

---

26 Just a little bit of celebrity spotting for you: Richard Raworth is the father of BBC newsreader Sophie Raworth. Not that I ever met her, but she doesn't seem nearly as scary as her dad.

table and then wait several weeks to see if the shareholders will accept it. You can't negotiate with individual shareholders; you have to make the same offer to them all at the same time. Everything needs to be in place before you make your offer – all the finance and due diligence – which means spending a lot of money before even knowing whether anyone intends to accept it. There's then an enforced wait of several weeks to allow competing bids to emerge. Experienced corporate predators cover themselves against this risk by building up a minority stake in secret to just short of the level that will trigger a full bid, meaning that, if they lose out to a higher bidder, at least their costs are covered by the profit they make on their shares. But that's also a risky strategy. If a higher bid doesn't materialise and your offer is deemed inadequate by the shareholders, all you've done is overpay for a minority stake in a moribund listed company.

There are traps all over the place; no wonder management buyouts of listed companies are extremely rare. It's clear that Campbell Lutyens have only approached 3i after trying and being rejected by pretty much every other VC in London. It looks hopeless.

David Hudson, who has to be the most resiliently optimistic adviser I have ever met, doesn't agree. If there were any other bidders, he contends, they would have emerged by now and, given we have the full cooperation of management, he doesn't see why assembling an offer needs to be difficult or expensive. He's prepared to put his money where his mouth is by working on a fully contingent basis[27] and has somehow persuaded a

---

27 In other words, he only gets paid if the bid succeeds.

reputable firm of experienced City solicitors to prepare all the necessary legal documentation on the same basis.

'What do you think?' he asks. 'Is 3i up for this?'

I think of Cul-de-Sac's wordy denunciation of the proposal, what an industrial adviser will think of the management team, what will happen when this gets presented to Investment Committee and how much work this could take with little guarantee of anything to show for it. I hate to admit it, but Cul-de-Sac has a point. Just getting it through is going to be tough enough. I'm also painfully conscious of the bloodlust throb in my veins to prove myself in London and get a deal done. Can I trust my judgement on this?

I look at Harold and catch his eye. He wants to do it, but his objectivity is as questionable as mine. If we do this and it goes wrong, my recent good run will be dismissed as beginner's luck. Moreover, we know this is a horse that has been widely touted around the market and on which not one single punter is willing to place a bet. If we take that bet and the horse falls at the first hurdle, we'll just look ridiculous. It all feels like a huge gamble.

For a moment the dark pit of prospective embarrassment and failure opens up beneath my feet and I see demons grinning up at me. On the other hand, the commercial logic *does* seem very sound and, if we can get it at the price we're proposing, it could be very good value. And I really do need to do a deal.

'Why not?' I say.

It's the critical moment. Harold and I are committed now and we keep plugging away until one by one the hurdles get removed or knocked down. Astonishingly, the deal actually starts to look like it's going to happen. The final hurdle is Investment Committee approval but, even though Cul-de-Sac is totally opposed to it, it goes through without much, if any, protest. It seems that IC now thinks I have the golden touch. That just makes it worse, really. Part of me wishes they had bounced it.

Finally the day comes when we take a deep breath and launch our formal offer. Stock Exchange rules require that the offer stay open for three weeks, during which time another buyer could emerge and outbid us. Even if that doesn't happen, there's no guarantee that the shareholders won't just deem our offer too low and ignore it, in which case we'll be landed with all the costs and a truly embarrassing amount of egg on our faces.

Twenty-one days and one minute later, David Hudson is on the telephone. We've called it all correctly and a sufficient majority of the shareholders has accepted our offer. It's only a £12m deal but I don't think 3i has ever done a public-to-private deal before. It's quite an achievement but I can't settle; I'm still haunted by Samji Industries. If this one goes wrong, it's back to witch-hunts and relegation to the Portfolio Team. In this business, no matter how many successes you have, you're only ever one deal away from being a fool.

Fortunately, the liberating effect on the business of being taken out from the defunct listing is remarkable, and both cash and profits race quickly ahead of forecast. Within three months, it's clear things are going well and we're likely to have another success on our hands.

The gamble pays off in another way. Suddenly, there are a few advisers who want my initials against theirs on the database. The deal famine eases.

Plaster Wig has long since been replaced as CEO by one of those Scotsmen who are very proud of their Scottish heritage while having been educated entirely at a private school in the

Home Counties. Humpty does the dour thing exceptionally well, though. It's not so much that he doesn't have a sense of humour as that he couldn't possibly fathom what on earth the purpose of such a frivolous thing would be. He's also terminally shy. This is long before emotional intelligence is seen as an essential component in the CEO toolkit.

Humpty has decided to commission a firm of consultants to review our culture. The point of this project is a little obscure but seems to be rooted in an article he read in *Fortune* about the world's Most Admired Companies. Humpty would like 3i to be regarded as a Most Admired Company, which is surprisingly sentimental for a man who sees no apparent role for feelings in business.

The team of consultants who descend on 3i are mostly psychotherapists on whom it has dawned that large companies pay much better than individuals suffering from low self-esteem, unsatisfying relationships or eating disorders. Somehow they persuade Humpty to put the entire company through a programme of psychotherapy, which involves each team being taken away for three days to learn how to express their inner feelings. Rather shrewdly, Humpty has the insight that the hard-bitten, deeply cynical controller stream might see this as all a bit too Dorothy. So, to give it some credibility, they ask a few of the controllers to get involved, including me. I am given some training in psychotherapy techniques, which prove remarkably similar to the methods for winning management teams over on a first meeting: show interest in the human story, be inquisitive, emphasise the positive and summarise frequently. I realise I would make an excellent psychotherapist, as long as the poor victim isn't actually expecting to get any better. As a general rule, you'd have to be a genuine lunatic to give *any* controller licence to rummage around in your head, helping himself or herself to whatever you've carelessly left lying around in there.

I am instructed that a good 'facilitator' (the corporate word for 'therapist') ought to commence every session by identifying his own state of mind and consciousness. The lead consultant elaborates for me:

'Personally, I begin each interaction with a moment of introspection … Am I feeling bored? Anxious? Distracted? Judgemental? Sexually aroused?'

Wait a minute. Did I hear that right? Did he just say, 'sexually aroused'?

'Yes, sexually aroused.'

OK. The word *inappropriate* seems appropriate.

'Just checking, but you didn't try that on Humpty did you?'

'Yes of course! All of the Exco members have been through the same training I'm giving you.'

'What? You told Exco they have to investigate their personal state of sexual arousal at the beginning of every meeting?'

The consultant is mystified. 'Yes of course. Why ever not?'

Brave.

It dawns on me that the consultant has just disclosed to me that he frequently begins meetings in a state of sexual arousal. If this is the case, I'm a little mystified as to why a whole process of introspection is required to make him aware of the fact. Perhaps he's capable of getting through an entire shag without noticing. I'm not sure if I'm shocked or impressed. I *am* sure that he is oversharing. Fortunately, he chooses not to elaborate on what typically provokes such a state or what remedies might be available should he discover, on introspection, that he has indeed started a meeting troubled by a distractingly urgent boner. I am also extremely grateful that this conversation takes place with his lower half concealed safely under the meeting room table.

Erections in meetings: the trouble is, this is not a thought I can now unthink. Hopefully you can't unthink it now either – a burden shared is a burden halved, after all.

I'm attending my first ever Investment Committee meeting.

It takes place in an ordinary meeting room on the tenth floor. Various directors drift in and there's an atmosphere like schoolchildren assembling in a classroom before the teacher arrives. There are lots of familiar characters here: Cul-de-Sac of course, Flagpole, the evil Lickspit, and even Cicero, who has recently become a regional director, plus some individuals with whom I am less familiar. Our finance director, Brian Larcombe, steals my notes and scribbles something derogatory on them in red pen before shoving them back across the table to me. When Humpty finally does appear, the class immediately puts its serious face on.

The deal I am presenting involves a company called Zotefoams and it's an MBO opportunity from BP. The business manufactures a specialised type of foam that is particularly useful in making toys, due to its stable and inert qualities. We've been through a beauty parade and are prepared to support the management team up to a valuation of about £20m. Three years ago, this would have seemed like a huge deal but now it's almost routine. We have already won the deal lead and an exclusivity agreement from BP. Investment Committee approval is the final stage before we commission due diligence and start legals.

It's always been a core principle that 3i doesn't invite Local Directors or controllers to attend Investment Committee. But enlightenment has dawned and LDs are now able to attend, present their deals and answer questions. It's a quiet revolution.

I am invited to give a brief (no more than two minutes, please) introduction and then Humpty goes around the table to solicit views. It's not a discussion and no one really asks a question. Again, it reminds me of a classroom where the teacher nominates various pupils to speak. The rules seem to be that you can't repeat what has already been said, you have to think of something original and you get extra points for concise, whip-smart points that demonstrate your shrewd commercial insight.

The role of the person chairing the meeting is critical. A good chairman will summarise the views expressed, give you a chance to respond and bring the discussion to a close by stating the outcome of the discussion – whether the deal has been approved and on what conditions, if there are any.

Humpty is not a good chairman.

As we go around the table, comments are made on everything: the technical specification of the product, the growth projections, the valuation, the personal qualities of the management team, the repayment profile of the preference shares and the key issues to focus on in the commercial due diligence. None of these points are picked up, clarified, developed or handed back to me for comment – they're just left dangling like old coats from pegs on a rack. Then Humpty takes off his own coat and hangs it up there with all the rest. He clears his throat and says there's a problem with the working capital.

I scramble through the pages of my Submission to get to the balance sheet and cashflow forecast, and quickly locate the working capital numbers. They look … well, completely normal. There *is* no problem with the working capital.

Humpty insists there is. I tell him there isn't. He glares at me and everyone around the table goes quiet. It's like a scene from a Western where two gunslingers face off while all the townspeople look on with bated breath.

Humpty clears his throat again, his eyes flick right and left. The sun beats down. In the distance a clock tower bell rings. A slow breeze whips up the sand around our feet and a knot of tumbleweed drifts past our stirruped boots. My hand twitches next to my holster and Humpty's wrist flicks in response. But since neither of us actually has a fully loaded Colt 45, it's hard to see how this stand-off is going to resolve itself.

'Well, there we have it,' Humpty says, then gathers his papers, gets up and leaves.

I resist the temptation to run after him flapping my elbows and squawking 'cluck cluck'.

I have no idea what just happened. Cicero comes over and suggests we wait for the minute to come out.

Later that day, the Committee minute appears and it says, 'Approved as submitted'. I must have been at a different meeting.

The deal completes and within six months management have released so much cash through tighter control of working capital that they are able to pay back a substantial portion of the MBO loan early. Within three years the company floats on the stock exchange at a valuation in excess of £50m.

So that's what happens at Investment Committee. Seems an odd way to arrive at an investment decision.

Managing people isn't quite as easy as I thought it would be. I am single-handedly proving my own theory that being good at deals is not a reliable guide as to who will make a good manager. I am given a team of four controllers and manage very skilfully to demotivate all of them completely within the first six months.

There's a tall, lanky lad whose arms seem to extend down to his knees. He's an Olympic-standard whinger and has absolutely no talent for the role at all. I tell him so and get told off by HR department. Apparently the correct procedure is to point out that there is a gap between where he is and where he needs to be.

There's a pompous, privately educated junior controller who has political connections at Westminster and who is clearly suffering from the impression that there has been a dreadful mix up: he should be the Local Director and I should be the junior controller. To prick his bubble, I make him sit on the private equity equivalent of the naughty step by sending him to the Zotefoams data room and telling him to read everything in it.[28] When he complains, I am unable to stop myself from sniggering.

My trainee is a lovely lad who has great potential but comes to me confessing that he's struggling with the anonymity and toxic politics of the London office. He's worried that he'll never get to work on any real deals and will just end up as an analyst. He's right, of course, so I sympathise and say I wouldn't blame him if he feels the need to leave, which he does.

The senior team member is a really pleasant, very experienced controller who has had a very good year. At the year end, I am delighted to see that he has been awarded a bonus and talk him up, saying how highly valued he is by the group, and so on and so forth. I hand over the cheque with a grand flourish, only to watch his expression change from optimism to disappointment.

---

28 When a company is up for sale, the owner typically fills up a 'data room' with just about every conceivable bit of information it can find, including insurance policies, health and safety records, property leases, asset finance agreements and any other old crap it can think of. The idea is to bury the poor purchaser under so much crap they give up before they get to the incriminating stuff, like the fact that the company has missed every single budget it has set itself for the last ten years.

It's only £500. He looks at me pityingly and asks if I realise he couldn't buy his wife a second-hand car with that.

Still, that's not quite as bad as one of the other Local Directors who is tasked with giving one of his controllers a startling 25% bonus. This is strange and rather annoying, as he doesn't rate the controller at all. Grudgingly, he summons the controller into his office to deliver the news, saying, ungraciously, he doesn't understand it himself but obviously someone upstairs has a higher opinion of the recipient than he does. When he hands over the cheque though, all he gets is a puzzled look. When he checks the schedule from HR he realises he's misread it: the bonus is not 25%; it's 0.25%.

When the year end comes around, both Zotefoams and Pron-taprint get big uplifts on valuation. Denby has weathered the recession well and there's even talk of a stock market flotation. The same is true of Nottingham Group. Teesside continues to storm ahead, with cash and profits stacking up faster than the containers being unloaded onto Tees & Hartlepool port wharves.

I'm happy to take the plaudits of course but, quietly, I'm as surprised as everyone else. I knew they were good businesses but I didn't anticipate these sorts of outcomes. Everyone seems to have forgotten about Samji and P K Stationery. Everyone, except me. I haven't forgotten at all, but I'm happy not to shatter the conspiracy of silence.

I receive a strange and unexpected summons to pay our CEO a visit. I confess I'm a little nervous in the lift – this is not at all usual. It occurs to me, inevitably, that I'm about to be told off about something. It would be deeply unfair but there are so many snide voices poisoning the London atmosphere that it wouldn't entirely surprise me.

When I enter his vast office on the tenth floor he is hunched behind his desk, an excellent panorama of London behind him. There are no preliminaries with Humpty; he just gestures towards the chair on the other side of his desk and clears his throat. He looks flushed and uncomfortable: you'd swear he'd been charged with telling me I had a dose of syphilis. Or body odour.

'Paul.'

Well, that's a good start. At least he got my name right.

He clears his throat again. That's twice now. 'The board wants to recognise the contribution you've made to the group.'

Oh, okay. This is unexpected. Where's he going with this?

'Accordingly, as a completely one-off gesture to reflect your achievements, the board has elected to award you a special bonus.'

Bloody hell! Now this is unexpected. Numbers start to cascade before my eyes, like he's just pulled the arm of a Las Vegas fruit machine in my head.

He clears his throat again. That's three times. Either there's an amphibian camped out in his larynx or he's deeply uncomfortable about something.

'I do need to stress that this is a one-off award only, and should in no way be seen as setting any kind of precedent.'

This must be a very big number. I think I'm actually holding my breath.

'The special bonus we have decided to award to you is £50,000.'

£50K?

Seriously?

Nowadays venture capital/private equity and personal wealth

are as inextricably linked as bread and butter, salt and pepper, champagne and caviar. As a way to achieve a personal net worth over £10m – or even £100m – venture capital and private equity are now well up there with becoming a hedge fund manager or a Russian gangster. But it wasn't always so. In 1985, nobody joined 3i in order to become seriously wealthy. My opening salary at 3i was £9,500, only a marginal increase on what I was earning at British Aerospace. Even five years in, as a senior controller in Nottingham, I was earning perhaps only £40k. Don't get me wrong – that's a handsome wage by any standards. But it didn't put me in a bracket where I could afford a second home in Cornwall, a yacht in Nice and a stake in a football club, nor did I have any savings or capital to my name.

The main reason why 3i is losing so many controllers to the competition is quite simply because they pay better. Salaries are higher, but the main point of difference is that all our competitors reward their investment executives with a share of deal profits, whereas 3i does not. We are not talking about tiny slivers of reward either; we're talking about big, fat, pizza-slices of dosh – like 20% of the profits.[29] Since the profit on a large MBO could well be £50m-£75m, 20% means we're talking serious

---

29 This has to be shared around the team but our competitors operate in small teams and the lion's share goes to the partners anyway. In addition, an independent private equity fund would charge its investors an annual fee of 2% of the size of the fund per annum. Sounds so modest, doesn't it? However, on a £300m mid-market buyout fund that would be £6m a year to sustain a team of only 8-10 executives. Moreover, it all adds up. Most private equity/VC funds have a fixed life of 10 years, so the *cumulative* fee would be not 2% but 20%, which gets deducted and paid from the total invested. So, within a £300m fund, only £240m is actually available for investment after allowing for the fees. In other words, the investments the team makes have to increase in value by £60m just to break even. And that's before taking account of the 20% of profits allocated to the carry scheme. Still think it's a modest arrangement? No, I didn't think so.

amounts of money for the individuals concerned. 3i refuses to compete with this for a whole range of quite honourable reasons: it thinks it distorts investment decision making, compromises teamwork and makes it hard to persuade controllers to move around between teams. But honour hath no skill in staff retention.[30]

If we ever bump into one another in real life, feel free to buy me a pint while I opine at length about the morality of this arrangement and the impact it has on the behaviour and attitude of investment executives. Fundamentally, in my view, the main effect of allowing investment executives to share in the capital profits of a deal is to boost, by a directly equivalent proportion, the ratio of an individual's self-esteem to their actual talent. But that's another story.

The point is that, whether it's justified or not, by the time I am having this awkward conversation with Humpty there are a lot of people in the industry doing exactly the same job as me and becoming seriously – and I mean *seriously* – wealthy as a result. In fact, since I have been obliged by my employer to routinely syndicate out the bulk of the investment, a number of these individuals are becoming very rich on the back of deals *I have led!* On a reasonable set of assumptions, had I been working for one of our competitors when I led the Nottingham Group, Denby, Teesside, Zotefoams and Prontaprint transactions, I could be expected to cash in a cheque of £5m, possibly more. I'm not saying I *deserved* a cheque for £5m, but I certainly could have expected to *earn* one.

This is the context in which you have to consider my reaction

---

30 Shamelessly nicked from William Shakespeare: "Honour hath no skill in surgery," *Henry IV.* Falstaff is unpersuaded to fight by appeals to his honour.

to Humpty's announcement of a special bonus of £50k. In my right ear, the good angel is telling me there are people who will not earn that amount in an entire lifetime – Duncan Gray, the assistant manager at Tesco's Gravesend superstore for one – and I should be immensely grateful. In my left ear, the bad angel is telling me I have just been deeply insulted.

Humpty clears his throat again. I don't think it's the inadequacy of the amount that is awkward for him. 'There is one condition. There's a clawback if you leave the group within the next twelve months.'

There's a reflective silence. I don't know what to say and neither does he. It's obvious what's been going on. It's occurred to someone that the competition are noticing my run of successes and are starting to hang around outside the school gate, dangling wads of fivers. So 3i has decided to dangle its own wad of fivers.

What Humpty naively doesn't realise is that the competitors' wads of fivers are much, much thicker than those he is waving. Or perhaps he does.

He clears his throat again but this time I think he means the interview is at an end.

It's ironic really. The gesture that is intended to secure my loyalty is actually the thing that triggers a process of self-reflection as to whether I should stay or go.

My elevation within the company has also been recognised by moving me out of the windowless office into one with a rather magnificent view. I close the door and stand for a while, looking out over the Thames. The river cruisers – flat, ugly little craft with their crop of well-fleeced tourists on board – brownnose their way against the indifferent tide. Down below, commuters pour out of Waterloo station like a river of ants, some gulped up by scarlet London buses while the rest scurry on and over Waterloo bridge. Across the river I can see the solid visage of Somerset House and, beyond that, the Houses of Parliament and Westminster Square. To my right, though much further away, a thicket of City skyscrapers glints in the early morning sun.

I won't lie to you – it's a nice feeling to be thought a great investor. Privately, I'm not so sure I possess any particular gift or special talent other than an ability to form a rapport quickly with management teams and a determination to find a way to get deals done. Despite the recession, the truth is that the management teams we are backing are still buying their businesses at a significant discount to what they are valued at by the market. Provided they don't collapse because you've loaded them with too much debt, you are almost certain to make money, not least because giving the management teams a big personal stake in their companies does focus them on delivering their budgets. The formula for success is therefore rather a simple one and doesn't require any particular brilliance: just find an MBO opportunity, win it, make sure the budgets are sensible and the team have a good track record, and give them as big an equity stake as you can get past your own, complaining organisation. It's a simple model and, by good fortune, I have found myself at the right time and in the right place to take advantage of it.

I think, too, that maybe I've finally solved the riddle of 'commercial judgement'. Or perhaps a better word is exposed it. When it comes to predicting company success, there's no particular talent involved: it's the simple law that states if lots of things can go wrong, then at least some of them (and probably most of them) will. Start-ups, early stage investing and small companies are tougher calls to make because, by definition, there is just so much that can go wrong. Buyouts, on the other hand, usually involve much bigger, more stable companies, so there's just less to go wrong. The easiest way to make money is to stick to buyouts. If you really want to do venture capital, well fine, but make sure there's plenty of upside in everything you touch because most of what you do will go wrong and you won't know which investments will succeed and which will fail until the fat lady actually stands up to sing. So 'commercial judgement' is not a mysterious metaphysical attribute – it's basic probability theory. Appreciating that requires humility, not vanity.

As for pricing, it's not science but religion. If everyone believes Jesus is the Son of God then, for all practical purposes, that's the same thing as it being true. If everyone believes that a price-earnings multiple above six is expensive for a foundry then, for all practical purposes, it is. But as with religious beliefs, it seems to be psychologically important for investors to believe pricing is anchored in some kind of metaphysical reality. The Protestant minister who thumps the pulpit and thunders that the Eucharist is not the Body of Christ does not believe he is expressing a mere social consensus – he thinks he is enlightening his congregation with a hard fact. What, essentially, is the difference between that and Warren Buffett claiming he can spot the intrinsic value of a company? Valuation is a matter of faith and expressions of faith call out for fervent assertion, not equivocation. Ambiguity and self-doubt paralyse; faith liberates and motivates. The price of a company is often established by nothing more concrete than how unequivocally it's asserted. There's nothing more persuasive than a person who passionately believes the bullshit they're peddling.

Valuing a company is not a scientific process; it's a theological one, dressed up as science. The trick is to work out the price available and then rationalise a way to justify it. Price-earnings ratios and discounted cashflow calculations are not scientific techniques; they're theological tools. Pricing, like religion, is a zeitgeist thing too. In 1620, everybody believed in witches, while in 2020 nobody does. The valuation zeitgeist evolves with sentiment and market conditions: the average price earnings ratio on the S&P 500 was under 5 in December 1920 and over 44 in December 1999. A change in the sea affects the worth of the fish. So commercial judgement is not about intuiting what the intrinsic value of a company is and comparing this to what less-talented mortals are pricing it at. It's about being the fish that knows when to join or leave the shoal.

I have very mixed feelings about 3i: it can be the most frustrating and infuriating place to work. But somehow it gets there in the end. It's true that I could make a lot more money elsewhere but even then, in the context of what most people earn, I am undeniably already – in my early thirties – extraordinarily well-paid. Even that special bonus can be read two ways: in the context of the market it's derisory, but in the context of 3i it's a genuine, almost affectionate, gesture.

There is a knock on my open door. It's Harold letting me know he wants a word.

'Well, fuck me sideways with a wet fish but it all seems to stack up.'

Conversations with Harold are invariably littered with deeply inappropriate, innuendo-rich mixed metaphors. He's been running the financial model on another deal we're looking at. It's far from the model I built on the laptop purchased with Cicero's company Barclaycard from the geeky computer shop on Bennetts Hill. That has long ago been superseded by a more sophisticated one written by a junior controller with real spreadsheet skills, and which has been distributed for use by all regional offices to ensure consistency across the group. How times have changed. But Harold has done a good job. We have a structure that works: realistic debt levels, a range of achievable bid valuations and an equity proposal to put to management. We still need to make the deal happen and there are at least a dozen obstacles to that, every one of which looks insurmountable at present. But then, as I said earlier, all deals are born drowning.

I think it's the people that keep me here. I'm not one of those business nerds who enjoys pulling apart businesses to see how they work, the way your dad liked dismantling the brake system on the family car with the Haynes manual open beside him. The truth is, I find the mechanics of commerce rather boring – it's the human stories I like. And I like the people I work with. Despite haemorrhaging experienced and capable people to the competition, 3i never fails to replace them with bright, ambitious young people. Which means it's a vibrant, youthful and fun place to spend your days (and sometimes your nights too). We are a close-knit community, a remarkable achievement in itself given how we're spread out across the UK in twenty different offices. Put a controller from Aberdeen together with one from Brighton and, even if they've never met before, within seconds they'll be sharing the same jokes, the same complaints and swapping war stories. Perhaps 3i is not so much a business as a family. You can't wait to leave but really you never do.

When I took that train to Birmingham six years ago, I had no idea what I was getting into and what the future held in store. It was as much a cack-handed attempt to manufacture an exit from a poor initial career choice as a decision to become a professional venture capitalist or private equity investor. I was raw, uneducated and, in commercial terms, positively bloody dangerous. Yet 3i had taken me in, tolerated me and even encouraged me. When by chance I stumbled into deals of real significance, 3i had been at first infuriatingly uncooperative; but, in being so, they taught me to fight and to win. It had also given me great times and great friends. For all the frustrations and peculiarities, I feel grateful for the opportunities the company has given me and gratitude does, at least in my case, entail loyalty. Well, up to a point …

On the other side of the river in the classy office suites of the West End, there are a dozen private equity firms who will pay me far better than 3i, give me more support and who are much better placed to exploit a market that is loping away to a bright future. These firms are designed for the MBO market At 3i, tilting at MBOs is like competing in a 100-metre sprint with your ankles tied to an industrial adviser whilst simultaneously pushing an uncooperative supermarket trolley loaded with several regional directors and the entire grudging complement of Investment Committee members. Rationally, it's a no brainer. But I'm just not feeling it. There are more deals here to be done and – here's a thought – imagine how good this place could be if only it was properly run.

I think I'm going to stick with it. A bit longer at least.

My reflective train of thinking is brought back to the conversation with Harold. He's telling me a long story about the birth of his second daughter involving a dash to hospital, a dose of irritable bowel syndrome, a McDonald's and a sympathetic midwife. But that's a story for another occasion …

Six months later I get another strange summons to go up and see Humpty. He still gives the impression he's about to tell me

I have syphilis and has to clear his throat three times before he broaches the subject he wants to talk to me about.

There's trouble in our French subsidiary. How do I feel about a secondment to Paris for a couple of years?

That's unexpected and my immediate instinct is to say 'no thanks'. After a rocky start, things are going well now in London and I know bugger all about the French market, except that it's all growth capital and there really is no management buyout market to speak of, which feels like a backward step. It's not at all clear what my role would be and my French is appalling. It's flattering to be asked but there's no doubt the sensible thing would be to stay where I am.

Sensible? What on earth am I thinking?

'Pourquoi pas?' I say.

ABOUT THE AUTHOR

Paul Traynor was born in Liverpool but grew up in Gravesend, in Kent. And, yes, the town really does deserve the name. He studied Philosophy, Politics and Economics at Oxford (not that there was *that* much studying going on) where his most impressive achievement was to learn to fly an aeroplane with the University Air Squadron. Ejected, rather grumpily, from Oxford when the course ran out, he joined British Aerospace on a graduate training scheme, where he became an expert at photocopying and finding tatty bedsits in depressed industrial areas. In 1985 he joined 3i as a trainee investment controller and stayed for fifteen years, spending time in Birmingham, Nottingham, London and Paris. In 1996 he was appointed Managing Director 3i Midlands, responsible for a team of thirty investment executives, which managed a portfolio of 550 investments valued in excess of £700m. He left 3i in 2000 confident that someone would soon offer him another extremely well-paid job. Shouldn't have to wait too much longer now. In the meantime, he keeps himself busy by making his superior blend of financial and industrial skills available on a consultancy basis to an assortment of venture capital and private equity firms, independent businesses and entrepreneurs.

Paul lives in south-west London with his wife and two teenage children.

ACKNOWLEDGEMENTS

My thanks go to Mark Heappey, Andy Stuart, Tim Farazmand, Mike France and John Bond of Whitefox Publishing for reading various drafts of the manuscript and offering invaluable advice and encouragement.

My thanks also to Jenny, Corry and Cassie for your insights and support with particular praise for Corry, who acted as my Head of Tomorrow in setting up the website and navigating me through the digital stuff.

Printed in Great Britain
by Amazon